P9-AFZ-338

COOKING IN SEASON

BRIGIT BINNS

PHOTOGRAPHY BY
RAY KACHATORIAN

weldon**owen**

CONTENTS

INTRODUCTION

Using Seasonal Ingredients 9

SPRING

Watermelon Radish Salad with Herbed Cheese,
   Blood Orange & Chives 18

Ricotta & Pea Crostini with Tarragon
   & Pink Peppercorns 20

Pan-Seared Halloumi with Fava Beans,
   Mint & Lemon 21

English Pea & Watercress Soup 23

Fresh Spring Rolls with Crab, Mango,
   Jicama & Haricots Verts 24

Clams in Leek Broth with Parsley Vinaigrette 25

Little Gem Salad with Shaved Carrot,
   Sunflower Seeds & Dill Vinaigrette 26

Black Lentil Salad with Shrimp, Green Garlic,
   Snap Peas & Moroccan Vinaigrette 28

Artichoke, Celery & Fennel Salad 29

Orecchiette with Spring Vegetables,
   Pecorino & Prosciutto 31

Swiss Chard & Spring Onion Frittata 32

Omelet-Soufflé with Spinach,
   Leek & New Potatoes 33

Spring Peas and Beans 34–35

Pan-Seared Salmon with Fresh Favas
   & Arugula Pesto 37

Seared Miso-Glazed Scallops with
   Snow Peas & Green Garlic 38

Sesame-Ginger Noodles with Peas,
   Shaved Asparagus & Radishes 39

Honey-Glazed Chicken Thighs with
   Rhubarb-Mint-Radish Slaw 40

Stir-Fried Beef with Asparagus, Bok Choy & Morels 42

Grilled Lamb Chops with Spring Herb Pesto 43

Pavlova with Meyer Lemon Curd & Strawberries 45

Kiwi & Passion Fruit Panna Cotta 46

Rhubarb-Ginger Crumble with Cardamom Cream 47

Naked Carrot Cake with Spring Blossoms 48

A Toast for Every Season 50–51

SUMMER

Summer Vegetable Ceviche 55

Peach Flatbread with Burrata,
   Arugula & Pickled Onion 56

Fried Squash Blossoms with Ricotta 57

Heirloom Tomato Tart 58

Blistered Padrón Peppers with Spicy Garlic Aioli 60

Golden Gazpacho with Torn Croutons
   & Cherry Tomato Salsa 61

Thai Beef Salad with Lemon Cucumber,
   Chile & Greens 63

Farro, Grilled Corn & Summer Squash Salad 64

Risotto with Fresh Corn & Basil Oil 65

Rice-Noodle Salad with Chicken,
   Summer Vegetables & Herbs 66

Stone Fruit Salad with Summer Lettuces,
   Hazelnuts & Goat Cheese 68

Watermelon, Nectarine & Mint Salad with
   Feta Cheese 69

Grilled Rib-Eye Steak with Avocado Chimichurri 71

Grilled Salmon with Stone Fruit–Herb Mojo 72

Zucchini Lasagna with Herbed Ricotta
   & Fresh Heirloom Tomato Sauce 73

Summer Fruits 74–75

Grilled Fish Tacos with Pineapple Salsa
   & Avocado Crema 76

Grilled Pork Chops with Summer Plums
   & Thyme 78

Pounded Chicken Breasts with
   Grilled Ratatouille 79

Blackberry & Blueberry Potpies 81

Apricot Pistachio Tart 82

Summer Cherry Clafoutis 83

Watermelon Mojito Pops 84

A Galette for Every Season 86–87

FALL

Creamy Parmesan Polenta with Wild Mushrooms 91

Fig, Blue Cheese & Walnut Crostini with
    Honey Drizzle 92

Smoky Eggplant Dip with Cumin-Crusted Pita Chips 93

Wheat Berry Salad with Chopped Chard,
    Pear & Sunflower Seeds 94

Coconut-Curry Butternut Squash Soup 96

Kale, White Bean & Sausage Soup 97

Seared Cauliflower Steaks with
    Olive-Caper Gremolata 99

Romaine & Roasted Delicata Squash Salad with
    Dates, Almonds & Bacon 100

Soft Tacos with Pumpkin, Black Beans
    & Avocado 101

Pappardelle with Romanesco & Kalamata Olives 102

Turmeric-Spiced Shrimp with Red Cabbage
    & Carrot Slaw 105

Chicken Tagine with Roasted Squash, Haricots Verts,
    Chickpeas & Cranberries 106

Turkey Breast with Chanterelle Ragout 107

Pork Skewers with Apple, Fresh Sage
    & Rustic Bread 108

Short Ribs with Carrot-Apple Purée 110

Roasted Pork Shoulder with Sweet Potatoes
    & Pomegranate 111

Pan-Seared Sea Bass with Acorn Squash 113

Autumnal Squashes 114–115

Cider-Braised Chicken Legs with Fresh Figs
    & Cipollini Onions 116

Apple Fritters with Cinnamon Cream 117

Pear, Quince & Apple Galette 119

Pumpkin Tart with Gingersnap Crust 120

Roasted Figs with Mascarpone 121

A Salad for Every Season 122–123

WINTER

Roasted Red & Yellow Beets with Burrata,
    Sherry Vinaigrette & Escarole 127

Roasted Oysters with Sriracha-Lime Butter 128

Crostini with Radicchio, Smoked Trout
    & Horseradish Cream 129

Creamy Cauliflower Soup with
    Brussels Sprout Hash 130

Oven-Roasted Ricotta with Citrus
    & Pomegranate 132

Potato & Pancetta Crostata with
    Fresh Rosemary 133

Parsnip Oven Fries with Chile-Spiced
    Crème Fraîche 135

Winter Vegetables 136–137

Mushroom Soup with Crispy Prosciutto
    & Marjoram 138

Crab Cioppino 139

Mixed Citrus Salad with Mâche, Fennel & Celery 140

Fuyu Persimmon Salad with Endive & Pomegranate 142

Warm Kale Salad with Lentils & Prosciutto 143

Pizza with Roasted Broccolini, Pancetta
    & Pine Nuts 145

Pasta with Brussels Sprout Leaves, Hazelnuts
    & Brown Butter 146

Chile-Spiced Halibut with Frisée & Tangerine Salad 147

Noodle Bowl with Soy-Glazed Duck,
    Shiitake Mushrooms & Winter Greens 148

Beef Tenderloin with Celery Root–Potato Purée 150

Five-Spice Pork Loin with Mango,
    Green Onion & Mint Salsa 151

Rack of Lamb with Spicy Cranberry Relish 153

Salted Caramel–Dipped Pears 154

Walnut Torte with Chocolate-Caramel Sauce 156

Pink Grapefruit Sorbet with Crystallized Ginger 157

Crème Brûlée with Caramelized Blood Oranges 158

A Cocktail for Every Season 160–161

PRODUCE IN SEASON 164
BASIC RECIPES 166
INDEX 169

INTRODUCTION

As a second-generation Californian, I learned from an early age to celebrate the seasons. When I was a kid, the arrival of spring excited me not (like my schoolmates) because it was almost swimming season, but because artichokes would soon be on my family's table—ideally, at least twice a week.

Back then (at least in urban Los Angeles), there were no wild mushrooms, no Romanesco broccoli, no multicolored beets. But we ate well and always in tune with the seasons because my mother—a great, if limited, cook—spent much of her youth on a cattle ranch near Santa Barbara. There, they grew their own vegetables and relied on twice-monthly forays to civilization for staples.

Annual summer visits to Connecticut allowed me to learn at the foot of a passionate vegetable gardener, the legendary mystery novelist and gourmand Rex Stout. "Have the water boiling before you pick the corn," he insisted, "then run from the plant to the pot." Rex's rustic grilled beef was legendary, and I still try to re-create it every summer.

Later, ten years in Europe exposed me to many fruits and vegetables than hadn't been available during my American upbringing. Six and a half years in England gave me a whole new appreciation for brussels sprouts and parsnips, but left me literally starved for bright, sunny food. The following three and a half years in Spain opened my eyes to the bounties of a warm-climate diet.

Then, somewhere along the way, I ended up in a rut. It was almost like the farmers' markets were for special occasions only; I stopped experimenting. Working on this book pushed me outside my comfort zone, and I fell in love with ingredients I'd only admired from afar—Delicata squash, watermelon radishes, Romanesco—and rekindled love affairs with forgotten foods: sweet potatoes, pomegranates, kiwifruit. It motivated me to think outside the box and invigorated my approach to dining both at home and in my cooking classes on California's Central Coast.

With this collection of recipes tailored to the seasons, you too will discover new flavors and inspiration, then create colorful (and healthy) meals using impeccably fresh produce for yourself and your family.

BUY LOCAL

Today, it's easier than ever to shop and eat locally and seasonally. But there's no need to insist that every single thing on your plate was grown within one hundred miles. As long as you make your best effort, you'll feel good on so many levels. The planet, your taste buds, and your health will all benefit.

CHECK RIPENESS

With some notable exceptions, most vegetables and fruits in the market should be ripe. Yet each has its own "secret handshake," and they are all worth learning. For example, when selecting pears, gently press near the top of the fruit around the stem; if it has any give at all, the pear is ripe. (By the time the side of the fruit feels soft, it's overripe inside.) Avocados are unusable until there is some "give" in their dark, knobby skin. Smaller fava bean pods yield little lime-green gems, barely in need of cooking, while beans from larger pods are best for braising.

STORE SMART

After you bring home the season's bounty, treat it with respect; your refrigerator is not the place for all produce. Tomatoes should never be refrigerated—it's a recipe for flavor loss. Leafy greens like chard, kale, and spinach must be kept chilled or they will wilt. Different members of the onion family go opposite ways: store leeks and green onions in the fridge, and red, yellow, and white onions on the counter or in a cool, dry pantry or cellar. (Rinse produce only when ready to use, never before storing in the refrigerator.)

COOK SEASONALLY

Many seasonal cooking techniques are no-brainers, especially if you live in a place where winter weather closes down the grill. That's when braising and roasting come to the rescue (think Cider-Braised Chicken and Pizza with Roasted Broccolini) and soups like Butternut Squash with Coconut Milk and Wild Mushroom Soup become lifesavers. In summer, much of the action is at the grill. Grilled Peach Flatbread with Burrata offers a rich marriage of flavors, but steaming or grilling vegetables and protein before the fierce heat arrives can also lead to even more summer-friendly repasts. I'm calm, cool, and collected when serving salads and chilled or room-temperature composed dishes like Summer Vegetable Ceviche and Blistered Padrón Peppers with Charred Lemon and Spicy Garlic Aioli.

SPRING

Market bins piled with bright green vegetables—peas, fava beans, asparagus, leeks, delicate lettuces—signal the arrival of spring. Cooking is quick and easy this time of year, with stir-fries, pan-seared seafood, and stove-top noodle dishes taking center stage.

Watermelon Radish Salad with Herbed Cheese, Blood Orange & Chives

Watermelon radishes, which thrive in cool spring weather, are large and round, which makes a V-slicer or mandoline the best tool for shaving them paper-thin. Either tool also makes quick work of reducing the jicama into uniform matchsticks.

FOR THE VINAIGRETTE

1 blood orange

1 shallot, minced

2 tbsp fresh lemon juice

⅛ tsp cayenne pepper

½ tsp salt

½ tsp freshly ground black pepper

¼ cup (60 ml) grapeseed oil

3 tbsp extra-virgin olive oil

2 blood oranges

½ small jicama, about ¾ lb (375 g), peeled and cut into ⅛-inch (3-mm) matchsticks

4 tbsp (½ oz/15 g) finely snipped fresh chives

1½ tbsp coarsely chopped fresh flat-leaf parsley

2 watermelon radishes, peeled and thinly shaved crosswise

9 oz (280 g) very cold goat cheese

serves 6

To make the vinaigrette, use a serrated knife to cut a thick slice off the top and bottom of the orange. Stand it upright and, following the contour of the fruit, carefully slice downward to remove the peel, pith, and membrane. Holding the fruit over a large, shallow bowl to catch the juices, cut on either side of each segment to free it from the membrane. Squeeze the membrane to release the juice into the bowl. Cut the segments crosswise into small pieces, discarding any seeds, and add to the bowl. Add the shallot, lemon juice, cayenne, salt, and black pepper. Whisking constantly, slowly add the grapeseed oil and olive oil and whisk until well combined.

Peel the remaining oranges as directed above. Set the fruit on its side and cut crosswise into slices ¼–½ inch (6–12 mm) thick, then cut the slices into halves, discarding any seeds. Add half of the blood oranges, the jicama, 2 tbsp of the chives, and the parsley to the bowl with the vinaigrette and toss well. Let stand for 5 minutes.

Arrange the salad on individual plates. Place the watermelon radish slices on top, then scatter with the remaining blood oranges and 2 tbsp chives. Crumble the goat cheese over the salads and serve.

A PALETTE OF RADISHES

If you can't find watermelon radishes, pick up a couple of bunches of crisp, mild, colorful Easter egg radishes, in a vivid mix of pink, crimson, deep purple, and white.

Ricotta & Pea Crostini with Tarragon & Pink Peppercorns

To ensure the peas are tender and sweet, purchase medium-size, firm, bright green pods and use them right away, before their sugars turn to starch. Slices from a whole-grain loaf rather than a baguette will give the crostini a more rustic flavor.

2 tbsp olive oil, plus more for brushing

1 green onion, sliced

1 tbsp sliced green garlic or 1 clove garlic, chopped

1½ cups (7½ oz/235 g) shelled English peas

1½ tbsp minced fresh tarragon, plus whole leaves for garnish

Salt and freshly ground pepper

¾ cup (6 oz/185 g) whole-milk ricotta cheese

½ cup (2 oz/60 g) grated Parmesan cheese

24 thin slices baguette

Crushed pink peppercorns for garnish

makes 24 crostini

Preheat the oven to 400°F (200°C).

In a frying pan, warm the olive oil over medium heat. Add the green onion and garlic and cook, stirring occasionally, until tender, about 1 minute. Add the peas and tarragon and stir to coat. Add ⅓ cup (80 ml) water, season with salt, and cook, stirring occasionally, until the peas are tender and almost all of the water has evaporated, about 7 minutes. Remove from the heat and let cool slightly.

Transfer to a food processor, add the ricotta and Parmesan, and process until smooth. Season to taste with salt and pepper. (The mixture can be covered and refrigerated for up to 2 days before continuing.)

Arrange the baguette slices on a large baking sheet. Brush the tops lightly with olive oil. Bake until lightly toasted, about 8 minutes.

Spread the toasts thickly with the pea purée and return to the baking sheet. Bake just until the purée is warmed through, about 7 minutes.

Arrange the crostini on a platter, sprinkle with pink peppercorns and tarragon leaves, and serve.

Pan-Seared Halloumi with Fava Beans, Mint & Lemon

Traditionally made from sheep's and goat's milk, halloumi is a firm and slightly springy brined cheese native to Cyprus that can be panfried or grilled without melting. Here, it adds rich flavor and creamy texture to quickly cooked fava beans.

Bring a small pot of generously salted water to a boil over high heat. Fill a bowl with ice water. Add the fava beans to the boiling water and cook for 3–5 minutes, depending on the size of the beans. Using a large wire skimmer or slotted spoon, transfer the beans to the ice water for 1–2 minutes, then drain. Squeeze each bean free of its tough outer skin. (The fava beans can be covered and refrigerated for up to 1 day.)

In a small bowl, whisk together 2 tbsp of the olive oil, ¼ tsp of the lemon zest, and the lemon juice until well combined. Season to taste with salt and set the vinaigrette aside.

In a frying pan, warm 1 tbsp of the olive oil over medium heat. Add the green onions and garlic and cook, stirring occasionally, until tender, about 1 minute. Add the fava beans and mint and stir to coat. Add ¼ cup (60 ml) water, cover, and cook until the fava beans are tender, about 4 minutes. Uncover, reduce the heat to the lowest possible setting to keep the beans warm, and season to taste with salt.

Meanwhile, sprinkle the cheese slices on both sides with the remaining ½ tsp lemon zest and the red pepper flakes. In a large nonstick frying pan, warm the remaining 1 tbsp olive oil over medium heat. Add the cheese in a single layer and cook, turning once, until golden brown on both sides, about 4 minutes total.

Spoon the fava beans onto a serving platter and arrange the cheese slices on top. Whisk the vinaigrette to recombine, then spoon over the cheese. Garnish with mint leaves and lemon wedges and serve.

Salt

1½ lb (750 g) fava beans in the pod, shelled

4 tbsp (60 ml) extra-virgin olive oil

¾ tsp grated lemon zest

1 tbsp fresh lemon juice

⅓ cup (1 oz/30 g) sliced green onions

2 cloves garlic, minced

⅓ cup (⅓ oz/10 g) fresh mint leaves, plus more for garnish

½ lb (250 g) halloumi cheese, cut into 8 slices

¼ tsp red pepper flakes

Lemon wedges for serving

serves 4

ADD A SWIRL

To create the pretty garnish
seen here, thin the crème
fraîche with a little water,
drizzle over the soup, then
drag the tip of a knife
through the crème to make
swirls. Finish each bowl
with a pea shoot tip.

English Pea & Watercress Soup

A trio of springtime favorites—peas, watercress, and green onions—imbues this soup with a beautiful emerald color. Slipping a russet potato into the pot gives the soup a smooth, velvety texture without the addition of cream.

In a large pot, warm the olive oil over medium-high heat. Add the green onions, garlic, and ginger and cook, stirring occasionally, until the green onions are tender, about 1 minute. Add the broth and potato and bring to a simmer. Reduce the heat to medium, cover, and cook until the potato is very tender, about 12 minutes. Stir in the watercress and peas, cover, and cook until the peas are tender, about 4 minutes. Remove from the heat and let cool slightly.

In a blender or food processor, working in batches if necessary, process the soup until smooth. Return the soup to the pot and whisk in the crème fraîche. (The soup can be cooled, covered, and refrigerated for up to 3 days.) Reheat the soup over medium heat until it just reaches a simmer. Season to taste with salt and pepper. Ladle the soup into warmed bowls, garnish with crème fraîche, and serve.

1 tbsp olive oil

⅔ cup (2 oz/60 g) sliced green onions

2 cloves garlic, chopped

1 tsp peeled and grated fresh ginger

5 cups (1.25 l) chicken broth

1 russet potato, peeled and cut into 1-inch (2.5-cm) chunks

4 cups (4 oz/125 g) watercress, leaves and tender stems only

3 cups (15 oz/470 g) shelled English peas

⅓ cup (3 oz/90 g) crème fraîche, plus more for garnish

Salt and freshly ground pepper

serves 4–6

Fresh Spring Rolls with Crab, Mango, Jicama & Haricots Verts

These colorful spring rolls offer a lovely mix of textures and hues. For a smooth assembly, prep all the ingredients before you start. Pour an aromatic white wine such as Sauvignon Blanc or Riesling to accompany the rolls.

1 tbsp peanut oil

2 tsp peeled and finely chopped fresh ginger

2 small cloves garlic, minced

¼ lb (125 g) haricots verts, trimmed and halved crosswise

½ lb (250 g) jumbo lump crabmeat, picked over for shell fragments

Wedge of jicama (about 3 oz/ 90 g), peeled and finely diced

6 green onions, thinly sliced

2 tbsp finely chopped fresh cilantro

1 mango, pitted, peeled, and coarsely chopped

12 large rice paper rounds, 8–9 inches (20–23 cm) in diameter

¼ cup (60 ml) fresh lime juice

2 tbsp piloncillo or dark brown sugar

2 tbsp fish sauce

1 tbsp rice vinegar

¾ cup (¾ oz/20 g) microgreens

makes 12 rolls; 24 bites

In a frying pan, warm the peanut oil over medium heat. Add the ginger and garlic and stir for 10 seconds. Add the haricots verts and cook, stirring constantly, until glossy and tender-crisp but still bright green, about 2 minutes. Remove from the heat and let cool before filling the rolls. (The haricots verts can be covered and refrigerated for up to 4 hours.)

In a bowl, stir together the crabmeat, jicama, green onions, and 1 tbsp of the cilantro. Fold in the mango until well combined.

On a work surface, set out a large, shallow bowl filled with water, a damp kitchen towel, the rice paper rounds, crab mixture, and haricots verts. Immerse a rice paper round in the water for 4–5 seconds, then place the round flat on the towel (the paper will become pliable and very delicate within a few moments). Spread about 2½ tbsp of the crab mixture in a rectangle across the center of the round, leaving a 2-inch (5-cm) uncovered border on either side. Lay a few haricots verts across the top of the filling. Roll the bottom edge of the round up to cover the filling, compacting it gently but firmly into an even cylinder. Fold in both sides and then continue rolling up toward the top edge, again compacting gently but firmly, to the end. Place, seam side down, on a large platter. Cover the roll with a damp paper towel and repeat with the remaining ingredients to make a total of 12 rolls. (Although best when freshly made, they can be made up to 2 hours ahead if covered with a clean, damp kitchen towel and refrigerated.)

In a small bowl, whisk together the lime juice, piloncillo, fish sauce, vinegar, and the remaining 1 tbsp cilantro until the piloncillo dissolves. Let stand for 5 minutes.

Using a sharp knife, cut each roll in half on the diagonal. Place, cut side up, on the platter. Transfer the dipping sauce to a small serving bowl and place in the center of the platter. Scatter with the microgreens and serve.

Clams in Leek Broth with Parsley Vinaigrette

You can use cockles or mussels in place of the clams in this recipe. Serve with crusty country-style bread to soak up the savory broth. The parsley vinaigrette is also delicious spooned over sliced grilled chicken or fish.

To make the vinaigrette, in a small bowl, whisk together the parsley, lemon zest and juice, olive oil, mustard, and garlic until well combined. Season with salt and pepper and let stand at room temperature.

In a large pot, melt the butter with the olive oil over medium heat. Add the garlic, leeks, and shallots and cook, stirring occasionally, until soft, about 5 minutes. Add the wine and cook for 2 minutes. Add the broth, raise the heat to medium-high, and bring to a boil. Add the clams, discarding any that do not close to the touch. Cover and cook until the clams have opened, 6–8 minutes. Discard any unopened clams.

Ladle the clams and broth into warmed bowls, drizzle with the vinaigrette, and serve.

FOR THE VINAIGRETTE

⅓ cup (½ oz/15 g) finely chopped fresh flat-leaf parsley

Grated zest and juice of 1 lemon

1 tbsp extra-virgin olive oil

1½ tsp Dijon mustard

1 clove garlic, minced

Salt and freshly ground pepper

1 tbsp unsalted butter

1 tbsp extra-virgin olive oil

2 cloves garlic, sliced

2 leeks, white and pale green parts, sliced

2 shallots, minced

½ cup (125 ml) dry white wine

1 cup (250 ml) chicken broth or clam juice

2 lb (1 kg) manila clams, scrubbed

serves 2–4

Little Gem Salad with Shaved Carrot, Sunflower Seeds & Dill Vinaigrette

Shaved carrots are light and colorful and mix easily with other lightweight ingredients, like the delicate, buttery leaves of Little Gem heads. The creaminess of the vinaigrette and the crunch of the sunflower seeds impart a subtle richness.

FOR THE VINAIGRETTE

6 tbsp (90 ml) extra-virgin olive oil

2 tbsp plus 1 tsp Champagne vinegar or white wine vinegar

1½ tsp Dijon mustard

1½ tbsp mayonnaise

1 shallot, minced

Salt and freshly ground pepper

2½ tbsp finely chopped fresh dill

4 heads Little Gem lettuce, about 12 oz (180 g) total, leaves separated

1 large carrot, peeled and shaved paper-thin

⅔ cup (1½ oz/45 g) sunflower seeds

Handful of nasturtium leaves and/or blossoms for garnish (optional)

serves 6

To make the vinaigrette, in a large bowl, whisk together the olive oil, vinegar, mustard, mayonnaise, shallot, ¾ tsp salt, and pepper to taste until well combined. Stir in the dill.

Add the lettuce, carrot, and half of the sunflower seeds and toss to combine. Scatter with the remaining sunflower seeds and some nasturtium leaves and/or blossoms, if using, and serve.

FLORAL EMBELLISHMENT

Nasturtiums or other
edible seasonal blossoms,
such as pansies, violets,
and marigolds, make a
colorful last-minute garnish
for springtime salads.

Black Lentil Salad with Shrimp, Green Garlic, Snap Peas & Moroccan Vinaigrette

Black lentils have an earthy quality that complements the briny shrimp and two favorites of the spring harvest—snap peas and green garlic—in this inspired salad. If desired, trade out the black lentils for the deep green Le Puy lentils of France.

FOR THE VINAIGRETTE

4 cloves garlic, minced

⅓ cup (⅓ oz/10 g) *each* **firmly packed fresh cilantro leaves and flat-leaf parsley leaves**

¼ cup (60 ml) fresh lemon juice

Salt

1½ tsp smoked paprika

¾ tsp ground cumin

⅛–¼ tsp cayenne pepper

½ cup (125 ml) extra-virgin olive oil

FOR THE LENTILS

1 tbsp extra-virgin olive oil

2 shallots, finely chopped

1 rib celery, finely chopped

1 large carrot, finely chopped

2 cloves garlic, minced

1½ cups (10½ oz/330 g) small black (beluga) lentils

2 cups (500 ml) chicken broth

Salt and freshly ground pepper

6 stalks green garlic

2 tbsp extra-virgin olive oil

½ lb (250 g) large shrimp (26–30 count), peeled and deveined, halved crosswise

7 oz (220 g) sugar snap peas

2 tbsp snipped fresh chives

serves 6

To make the vinaigrette, in a food processor, combine the garlic, cilantro, parsley, lemon juice, 1 tsp salt, paprika, cumin, cayenne, and olive oil and pulse until smooth. Refrigerate until ready to serve, up to 3 hours.

To make the lentils, in a large saucepan, warm the olive oil over medium-low heat. Add the shallots and cook, stirring occasionally, until softened, about 4 minutes. Add the celery and about three-fourths of the carrot and cook, stirring occasionally, until softened, 3–4 minutes. Add the garlic and stir for 1 minute. Add the lentils and stir to coat with the oil, then add the broth and ¾ cup (180 ml) water; the lentils should be covered by about ¼ inch (6 mm) of liquid. Bring to a boil over medium-high heat, then reduce the heat to medium-low, partially cover the pan, and simmer gently for 15 minutes. Stir in the remaining carrot and cook until the lentils are tender but firm to the bite, about 10 minutes longer. Season to taste with salt and pepper.

Remove the lentils from the heat and let stand, covered, for 5 minutes. If there is a lot of excess liquid, drain the lentils in a fine-mesh sieve. While the lentils are still hot, combine them with a generous amount of the vinaigrette, reserving the remaining vinaigrette for the table. (At this point, the lentils can be cooled and stored in an airtight container in the refrigerator for up to 2 days; bring to room temperature before continuing.)

Thinly slice the green garlic on the diagonal. In a large frying pan, warm the olive oil over low heat. Add the green garlic and cook gently, stirring occasionally, until tender, 5–6 minutes. Raise the heat to medium-high and when the pan is hot, add the shrimp and snap peas. Cook, stirring constantly, until the shrimp are firm and pink and the snap peas are tender-crisp, 2–3 minutes.

Immediately spoon the shrimp mixture, including the juices, over the lentils and toss gently to mix. Sprinkle with the chives and serve.

Artichoke, Celery & Fennel Salad

Fresh artichokes seem like a bit of work, but the flavorful result is well worth the effort. Select artichokes that feel firm and heavy for their size, have tightly packed leaves, and emit a squeak when squeezed—a signal they were recently picked.

To make the dressing, in a large bowl, whisk together the vinegar, mayonnaise, olive oil, sour cream, mustard, oregano, salt, and pepper until well combined. Set aside.

Working with 1 artichoke at a time, cut off the stem flush with the bottom. Snap off the dark outer green leaves until you reach the tender yellow inner leaves. Discard the outer green leaves. Cut about 1 inch (2.5 cm) off the top of the artichoke. With a sharp paring knife, carefully trim away the remaining dark green bits all the way around the heart. Scrape out and discard the choke (a melon baller is useful here). Cut each heart into ⅛-inch (3-mm) slices and squeeze some lemon juice over them to prevent browning.

In a large frying pan, melt the butter with the olive oil over medium-low heat. Add the hearts and cook, stirring frequently, until softened and lightly browned, 7–9 minutes. Transfer to a bowl and let cool.

Add the fennel, celery, and half of the cheese to the bowl with the dressing and toss to coat. Divide the salad among individual plates and top with the artichokes and remaining cheese, dividing evenly. Scatter with a few oregano blossoms, if using, and serve.

FOR THE DRESSING

2 tbsp white wine vinegar

2 tbsp mayonnaise

2 tbsp extra-virgin olive oil

2 tbsp sour cream

1 tsp Dijon mustard

2 tsp minced fresh oregano

½ tsp salt

¼ tsp freshly ground pepper

4 large artichokes, about 1½ lb (680 kg) total

1 lemon, halved

1 tbsp unsalted butter

1 tbsp extra-virgin olive oil

2 large fennel bulbs, trimmed, quartered, cored, and very thinly sliced crosswise

4 or 5 large, pale inner ribs celery, very thinly sliced crosswise

¾ cup (4 oz/125 g) crumbled feta cheese

Oregano blossoms for garnish (optional)

serves 4–6

SWAP SIMILAR INGREDIENTS
You can substitute crisp, sweet sugar snap peas, another common harvest of the spring legume garden, for snow peas in nearly any recipe.

Orecchiette with Spring Vegetables, Pecorino & Prosciutto

In Italy, pasta or rice simmered in wine, usually red, is described as *ubriaco*, or "drunken." Here, a white wine finish lends the orecchiette a lovely perfume. Use good-quality wine and pour the same label at the table.

In a small bowl, using a fork, mash together the butter, lemon zest, ½ tsp salt, and a generous grinding of black pepper. Refrigerate until ready to use.

Bring a large pot of salted water to a boil over high heat. Fill a bowl with ice water. Cut the asparagus spears into 1½-inch (4-cm) lengths, keeping the stalks and tips separate. Add the stalks to the boiling water and cook for 1 minute. Add the tips and the snow peas and cook for 1½ minutes. Using a large skimmer, transfer the vegetables to the ice water. Drain and pat dry with a kitchen towel. Reduce the heat to keep the cooking water at a simmer for the pasta.

In a large sauté pan, warm the olive oil over medium heat. Add the shallot, prosciutto, garlic, and red pepper flakes and cook, stirring occasionally, until the garlic is softened, about 2 minutes. Add the wine and adjust the heat so the liquid simmers very gently.

Bring the water to a boil over high heat. Add the pasta and cook just until it starts to become flexible, about 5 minutes. Using a wire skimmer or slotted spoon, transfer the pasta to the sauté pan, raise the heat to medium-high, and cook, stirring frequently, until most of the wine has evaporated and the pasta is al dente, about 6 minutes. Add the asparagus, snow peas, and herbs and cook, stirring occasionally, until warmed through, about 2 minutes.

Remove the pan from the heat. Add the lemon butter and ¼ cup (1 oz/30 g) of the cheese, stirring until they have formed a rich glaze.

Divide the pasta among warmed bowls. Sprinkle with the remaining ¼ cup (1 oz/30 g) cheese and the garlicky bread crumbs and serve.

4 tbsp (2 oz/60 g) salted cultured butter, at room temperature

Grated zest of 1 lemon

Salt and freshly ground black pepper

25 thin asparagus spears, about 1 lb (500 g) total, tough ends snapped off

¼ lb (4 oz/125 g) snow peas, trimmed and halved lengthwise

1 tbsp olive oil

1 large shallot, finely chopped

¼ lb (4 oz/125 g) thinly sliced prosciutto, slivered

3 cloves garlic, minced

¼ tsp red pepper flakes

3 cups (24 oz/750 ml) medium-bodied white wine, such as Viognier or a rich Sauvignon Blanc

1 lb (16 oz/500 g) orecchiette

3 tbsp chopped mixed fresh herbs, such as parsley, oregano, and chives

½ cup (2 oz/60 g) grated pecorino cheese

½ cup (¾ oz/20 g) Garlicky Bread Crumbs (page 100)

serves 4–6

Swiss Chard & Spring Onion Frittata

More sharply flavored and with a larger, more bulbous base, spring onions are green onions that have grown up a bit but are not yet bulb onions. They can be red or white, depending on the varietal.

1 bunch green Swiss chard, about 1¼ lb (625 g)

4 tbsp (60 ml) olive oil

2 spring onions, thinly sliced

Salt and freshly ground black pepper

6 large eggs

4 cloves garlic, minced

¼ cup (1 oz/30 g) grated Parmesan cheese

1 or 2 pinches cayenne pepper

serves 4–6

Place a rack in the upper third of the oven and preheat to 350°F (180°C).

Separate the stems from the chard leaves by cutting along both sides of the center vein. Cut the stems crosswise into slices ¼ inch (6 mm) thick and coarsely chop the leaves. Set aside separately.

In a large frying pan, warm 2 tbsp of the olive oil over medium heat. Add the onions and cook, stirring occasionally, until tender, about 6 minutes. Add the chard stems, season with salt, and cook, stirring occasionally, until they start to soften, about 4 minutes. Add the chard leaves and cook, stirring occasionally, until all of the chard is tender, 3–4 minutes longer. Transfer to a plate and set aside.

In a large bowl, lightly beat together the eggs, garlic, and cheese. Season with the cayenne, salt, and black pepper. Drain the liquid from the plate holding the chard, squeeze the leaves gently to remove any excess liquid, and stir the leaves and stems into the egg mixture.

In a small nonstick ovenproof frying pan, warm the remaining 2 tbsp olive oil over medium-high heat. Add the egg mixture, reduce the heat to medium, and cook without stirring until the eggs are set around the edges, about 5 minutes. Transfer to the oven and bake until completely set, 7–9 minutes. Let cool briefly.

Cut the frittata into wedges and serve directly from the pan. Alternatively, invert the frittata onto a large plate, cut into wedges, and serve.

Omelet-Soufflé with Spinach, Leek & New Potatoes

This inspired soufflé–omelet hybrid is less demanding to make than a soufflé and equally impressive. To change up the flavors, substitute 6 oz (180 g) smoked salmon for the potatoes, ramps for the leeks and spinach, and dill for the chives.

In a steamer basket set over a large saucepan of simmering water, cover and steam the potatoes until tender, about 20 minutes. When the potatoes are cool enough to handle, quarter them lengthwise, then cut the quarters crosswise into slices ¼ inch (6 mm) thick.

Preheat the oven to 350°F (180°C).

In a large frying pan, melt 1 tbsp of the butter over medium-low heat. Add the leek and cook, stirring occasionally, until tender, about 5 minutes. Remove from the heat, add the spinach, and cover the pan. Let stand to wilt the spinach, about 5 minutes.

In a large, perfectly clean bowl, using an electric mixer, beat the egg whites, cream of tartar, and ⅓ cup (80 ml) water on high speed until stiff but not dry (the whites should not slip when the bowl is tilted).

In another bowl, using an electric mixer, beat the egg yolks and ¾ tsp salt on medium speed until slightly pale and thickened, about 1 minute. Stir in the spinach mixture, cheese, cream, ¼ tsp pepper, and 2 tbsp of the chives until well combined. Gently but thoroughly fold the yolk mixture into the egg whites, working quickly and maintaining as much air in the mixture as possible.

In a large ovenproof nonstick frying pan, melt the remaining 1 tbsp butter over medium-high heat. When the foam subsides, gently scoop the egg mixture into the pan and smooth the surface. Scatter the potato pieces evenly on top. Reduce the heat to medium and cook until the omelet is puffed and firm and the sides are golden, 6–7 minutes. Transfer to the oven and bake until the omelet is firm in the center and slightly golden on top, 9–10 minutes.

Let the omelet rest for 2–3 minutes, then sprinkle with the remaining 2 tbsp chives. Using a nonstick spatula, cut and serve large wedges directly from the pan.

5 small new potatoes, about ¾ lb (12 oz/350 g) total

2 tbsp unsalted butter

1 large leek, white and pale green parts, finely chopped

4 cups (4 oz/125 g) packed baby spinach leaves, coarsely chopped

8 large eggs, separated

¾ tsp cream of tartar

Salt and freshly ground pepper

1 cup (4 oz/125 g) grated Gruyère cheese

2 tbsp heavy cream, crème fraîche, or sour cream

4 tbsp (⅓ oz/10 g) finely snipped fresh chives

serves 4

SUGAR SNAP PEAS

SNOW PEAS

Spring Peas and Beans

The season's peas come in two types,
shelling and pod. English peas—aka
garden peas—must be freed from their
inedible pods before cooking, while flat,
sleek snow peas and crunchy sugar snaps
are eaten pod and all. Pea shoots, the leaves,
tendrils, and occasional blossom harvested
from the tip of a pea plant, are delicious
raw or lightly cooked. Fava beans must be
shelled and then each bean peeled—a task
that is time-consuming but worth it.

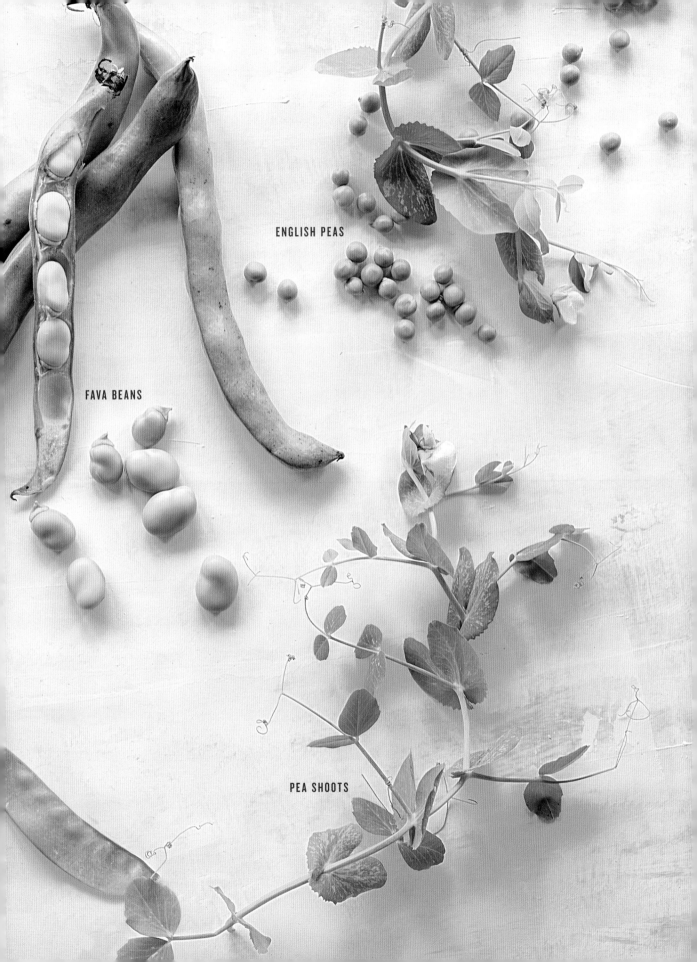

ENGLISH PEAS

FAVA BEANS

PEA SHOOTS

MELLOW WITH MINT

Most baby arugula is pleasantly peppery, but if what you find is too sharply flavored for this pesto, use three parts arugula and one part fresh mint leaves.

Pan-Seared Salmon with Fresh Favas & Arugula Pesto

Fava beans have a limited season, so scoop them up when you see them. You must work to enjoy these jade green gems, first slipping them from their pods, then peeling away the skin from each bean, but their unique grassy flavor is worth the effort.

To make the pesto, in a food processor, combine the garlic, pine nuts, arugula, olive oil, ½ tsp salt, and ½ tsp pepper and pulse until almost smooth. Set aside.

Bring a large pot of generously salted water to a boil over high heat. Fill a bowl with ice water. Add the fava beans to the boiling water and cook for 3–5 minutes, depending on the size of the beans. Using a large wire skimmer or slotted spoon, transfer the beans to the ice water for 1–2 minutes, then drain. Squeeze each bean free of its tough outer skin. (The fava beans can be covered and refrigerated for up to 1 day.)

In a sauté pan, melt 1 tbsp of the butter with the olive oil over medium heat. Add the fava beans and season with salt and plenty of pepper. Sizzle until the beans are warm and take on a little color, 1–2 minutes. Transfer to a baking dish and keep warm.

Pat the fish fillets dry with paper towels and season lightly on both sides with salt and pepper. In a large cast-iron frying pan or clean sauté pan, melt the remaining 1½ tbsp butter with the grapeseed oil over medium-high heat. When the foam subsides and the butter is just beginning to brown, swirl the pan to coat it evenly. Quickly add the fillets and cook without moving them until the edges begin to turn opaque, about 3 minutes. Gently turn the fish over and cook until just firm to the touch and opaque at the center, 2–3 minutes longer.

Place a fish fillet on each individual serving plate, top with the pesto and fava beans, and serve.

FOR THE ARUGULA PESTO

4 cloves garlic, minced

3 tbsp pine nuts, toasted

4 cups (4 oz/125 g) lightly packed baby arugula

½ cup (125 ml) extra-virgin olive oil

Salt and freshly ground pepper

Salt and freshly ground pepper

4 lb (2 kg) fava beans in the pod, shelled

2½ tbsp unsalted butter

1 tbsp extra-virgin olive oil

6 salmon fillets or sea bass fillets, 6–7 oz (185–220 g) each and about 1¼ inches (3 cm) thick

2 tsp grapeseed or canola oil

serves 6

Seared Miso-Glazed Scallops with Snow Peas & Green Garlic

Be sure the pan is superhot before you add the scallops. That way, they will be nicely browned and crisp on the exterior and tender and moist at the center. This recipe cooks quickly, so have everything at hand before you start.

FOR THE GLAZE

6 tbsp white miso

¼ cup (60 ml) mirin or sake

1 tbsp honey

4 tsp firmly packed golden brown sugar

2 tsp soy sauce

Freshly ground pepper

1¼ lb (600 g) large sea scallops, patted dry

4 tsp grapeseed oil

1 tbsp unsalted butter

½ cup (1½ oz/40 g) sliced green onions

¼ cup (¾ oz/20 g) thinly sliced green garlic

12 oz (350 g) snow peas, trimmed

½ cup (125 ml) dry white wine

2 tsp honey

Salt and freshly ground pepper

serves 4

To make the glaze, in a small saucepan, combine the miso, mirin, honey, brown sugar, and soy sauce. Place over medium-low heat and whisk until the sugar dissolves, then continue to cook, stirring occasionally, until slightly reduced and thick enough to coat the back of a spoon, 3–4 minutes. Season with pepper. Transfer to a large bowl and let cool.

Add the scallops to the glaze and toss to coat. Heat a large frying pan over high heat. When the pan is hot, drizzle in the grapeseed oil, turning the pan to coat it with the oil. Add the scallops and sear, turning once, until well browned on both sides and just barely cooked in the center, about 3 minutes total. Transfer the scallops to a plate.

Reduce the heat to medium-high and add ½ tbsp of the butter to the pan. Add the green onions and green garlic and cook, stirring occasionally, until tender, about 30 seconds. Add the snow peas and stir and toss until tender-crisp, 1–2 minutes. Divide the snow peas among 4 individual serving plates.

Pour the wine into the pan and bring to a boil, stirring to scrape up any browned bits from the pan bottom. Whisk in the honey and the remaining ½ tbsp butter, and season with salt and pepper.

Arrange the scallops over the peas on each plate, drizzle with the pan sauce, and serve.

Sesame-Ginger Noodles with Peas, Shaved Asparagus & Radishes

Nearly every cuisine has its own noodle salad. Here, I've married ingredients from kitchens in the East and West to create a robustly flavored vegetarian noodle salad that can be served warm, as here, or at room temperature.

Bring a large pot of lightly salted water to a boil over high heat. If using fresh peas, add them to the water and blanch for 1 minute, scoop out with a fine-mesh sieve, rinse with cold water, and set aside. If using thawed peas, skip this step.

Add the noodles to the boiling water, breaking up any clumps. Cook until just tender but still slightly firm, about 4½–5 minutes for egg noodles and 3–4 minutes for angel hair noodles. Drain and rinse well with running cold water, then drain again. Transfer the noodles to a large, shallow bowl, quickly drizzle with the sesame oil, and toss well to prevent them from sticking together. Stir in the peas. Cover and refrigerate for at least 30 minutes or up to 4 hours.

Using a sharp vegetable peeler and starting at the stem end, shave the asparagus into long, thin ribbons. Set aside.

To make the dressing, in a bowl, whisk together the tahini, vinegar, lime juice, soy sauce, peanut oil, brown sugar, ginger, garlic, red chili paste, and ½ tsp salt, then whisk in ¼ cup (60 ml) hot water until well combined.

Drizzle the dressing over the noodles and add about three-fourths each of the asparagus, bean sprouts, and radishes. Using tongs, toss until well combined. Scatter the remaining vegetables, sesame seeds, and mint on top and serve.

Salt

2 cups (10 oz/315 g) shelled English peas or thawed frozen peas

¾ lb (375 g) fine dried Chinese egg noodles or angel hair noodles

3 tbsp toasted sesame oil

6 large asparagus spears, tough ends snapped off

FOR THE DRESSING

¼ cup (2 oz/60 g) tahini

¼ cup (60 ml) rice vinegar

3 tbsp fresh lime juice

3 tbsp soy sauce

2 tbsp peanut oil

2 tbsp firmly packed dark brown sugar

2½ tsp peeled and minced or grated fresh ginger

3 cloves garlic, minced

1½ tsp red chili paste

Salt

2 cups (6 oz/200 g) bean sprouts

12 radishes, julienned

1½ tbsp black sesame seeds

3 tbsp coarsely chopped fresh mint

serves 6

Honey-Glazed Chicken Thighs with Rhubarb-Mint-Radish Slaw

If honey begins to crystallize, it can be difficult to blend with thinner liquids. To solve the problem, set the container in a pan of barely simmering water or in a microwave on low power for 5-second bursts until it is easily pourable.

12 bone-in, skin-on chicken thighs, about 4½ lb (2.25 kg)

Extra-virgin olive oil for brushing

1½ tsp ground cumin

Salt and freshly ground pepper

FOR THE GLAZE

3 tbsp honey

1 tbsp extra-virgin olive oil

1 tbsp fresh lemon juice

1 shallot, minced

FOR THE SLAW

⅓ cup (80 ml) extra-virgin olive oil

1½ tbsp fresh lime juice

1 tbsp honey

Salt and freshly ground pepper

⅓ cup (⅓ oz/10 g) coarsely chopped fresh mint, plus a few whole leaves for garnish

5–6 rhubarb stalks (about 11 oz/345 g total), trimmed and very thinly sliced on the diagonal

6 radishes, finely julienned

serves 6

Line a rimmed baking sheet with aluminum foil and place a flat wire rack on top.

Pat the chicken thighs dry with paper towels. Make 2 deep slashes on the skin side of each thigh, cutting down to the bone. Coat the chicken lightly on both sides with olive oil, sprinkle with the cumin, and season generously with salt and pepper. Place on the rack-lined baking sheet, cover with a paper towel, and let stand at room temperature for 1 hour.

Preheat the oven to 375°F (190°C).

To make the glaze, in a small bowl, whisk together the honey, olive oil, lemon juice, and shallot. Set aside.

Uncover the chicken, transfer to the oven, and roast for 12 minutes, then spoon some of the glaze over each thigh. Continue to roast until the skin is golden brown and an instant-read thermometer inserted into the thickest part of a thigh, away from the bone, registers 160°F (71°C), 10–12 minutes longer.

Meanwhile, make the slaw: In a medium bowl, whisk together the olive oil, lime juice, honey, ¼ tsp each salt and pepper, and three-fourths of the chopped mint until well combined. Fold in the rhubarb and radishes. Sprinkle with the remaining mint and whole mint leaves and serve alongside the chicken.

EMBRACE TARTNESS
Rhubarb can be quite
tart, so slice it paper-thin,
ideally with a mandoline,
and balance its acidity
with sweet and rich flavors.

Stir-Fried Beef with Asparagus, Bok Choy & Morels

As a college student in the Chinese Studies department, I loved everything about China except the cooking. It called for too much last-minute chopping! I changed my mind once I discovered that most of the work is best done in advance.

1 lb (500 g) rib-eye steak, trimmed of excess fat

Salt and freshly ground pepper

2 heads baby bok choy

5 green onions

2 tbsp sambal oelek or red chili paste

1½ tbsp peeled and minced or grated fresh ginger

1 tbsp toasted sesame oil

1 tbsp rice vinegar

1 tbsp fresh lime juice

1½ tsp fish sauce

3 tbsp peanut or grapeseed oil

30 thin asparagus spears, about 1 lb (500 g) total, tough ends snapped off, spears cut crosswise into 2-inch (5-cm) lengths

½ lb (250 g) fresh morel mushrooms, stemmed and brushed clean, or shiitake mushrooms, stemmed and sliced

4–5 oz (125–155 g) pea shoots

serves 4

Pat the steak thoroughly dry with paper towels, then freeze the steak for 25 minutes (this will make it easier to slice). Cut the steak across the grain into ¼-inch (6-mm) slices and season generously with salt and pepper.

Cut the bok choy in half crosswise just above the white part. Quarter, core, and sliver the white parts. Coarsely chop the upper green leaves, keeping the white parts separate from the green leaves. Finely chop the green onions, keeping the white parts separate from the green parts. Set aside.

In a small bowl, whisk together the sambal oelek, ginger, sesame oil, vinegar, lime juice, fish sauce, and ¼ tsp salt until smooth. Set aside.

Have all of the ingredients assembled by the stove top. In a wok or very large frying pan, warm 2 tbsp of the peanut oil over high heat until very hot, 2–3 minutes. Add the white parts of the bok choy, spread around the wok, and let sizzle for 1 minute. Stir in the asparagus and mushrooms, spread them out in the wok, and cook, tossing about every 45 seconds, until slightly softened and glossy, 3–4 minutes. Add the white parts of the green onions and toss for 1 minute. Scrape the vegetables onto a platter and quickly wipe out the wok with a paper towel.

When the wok is very hot again, pour in the remaining 1 tbsp peanut oil and swirl. Add the beef, distributing it evenly so that all the pieces are in contact with the hot surface, and let sizzle without disturbing until golden brown, about 1 minute. Return the vegetables to the wok and add the pea shoots, bok choy leaves, and the sambal oelek mixture. Reduce the heat to medium and toss to blend the flavors and warm through, 1–2 minutes. Scatter the green parts of the green onions on top and serve.

Grilled Lamb Chops with Spring Herb Pesto

The term *spring lamb* was traditionally used for animals born in winter and brought to market in spring. Nowadays, it usually indicates the animal's age (six to twelve months) rather than the market season. Lamb remains a popular spring menu choice.

Prepare a grill for direct-heat cooking over high heat.

To make the pesto, in a food processor, combine the basil, parsley, mint, almonds, garlic, and 1 tsp salt and process until coarsely chopped, stopping to scrape down the sides of the bowl as needed. With the motor running, drizzle in the olive oil and purée to a thick consistency. Scrape the pesto into a bowl and stir in the vinegar. Set aside.

Rub the lamb chops on both sides with the olive oil and season all over with salt and pepper. Place the chops on the grill rack and grill, turning once, until seared, nicely grill-marked, and medium-rare, about 6 minutes total. Transfer to a platter, tent with aluminum foil, and let rest for 5 minutes.

Place 2 chops on each of 4 individual plates, spoon a generous dollop of pesto on the side, and serve.

FOR THE PESTO

1½ cups (1½ oz/45 g) lightly packed fresh basil leaves

1 cup (1 oz/30 g) lightly packed fresh flat-leaf parsley leaves

½ cup (½ oz/15 g) lightly packed fresh mint leaves

3 tbsp slivered almonds, lightly toasted

2 cloves garlic, chopped

Salt

¾ cup (180 ml) extra-virgin olive oil

2 tsp red wine vinegar or white balsamic vinegar

8 lamb rib or loin chops, each about 1 inch (2.5 cm) thick

2 tbsp extra-virgin olive oil

Salt and freshly ground pepper

serves 4

THE BEAUTY OF MEYER LEMONS

Sweeter than the more common Lisbon or Eureka lemon, Meyer lemons arrive in markets in late November and remain through spring, perfect timing for this sweet-tart curd.

Pavlova with Meyer Lemon Curd & Strawberries

This meringue dessert, named for the Russian ballerina Anna Pavlova, has a crisp crust and soft, chewy interior that makes an excellent backdrop for the first berries of the season. Berry blossoms and leaves make an especially lovely garnish.

To make the lemon curd, have ready a large bowl filled with ice water. In a nonreactive saucepan, whisk together the eggs, egg yolks, and sugar. Whisk in the lemon zest, lemon juice, and salt. Place over low heat and cook, whisking constantly, until the mixture turns bright yellow and is thick enough to coat the back of a wooden spoon, about 7 minutes. Do not boil. Remove the pan from the heat and whisk in the butter. Strain the mixture through a fine-mesh sieve into a clean bowl and nest the bowl in the ice water. Whisk occasionally until the lemon curd is completely cool. Transfer the curd to a smaller container, cover, and refrigerate until completely cold, about 2 hours.

Place a rack in the lower third of the oven and preheat to 300°F (150°C). Draw a 9-inch (23-cm) circle on a sheet of parchment paper. Turn the parchment paper over and place on a baking sheet.

In a bowl, using an electric mixer, beat the egg whites on medium speed until well mixed. Sprinkle the cornstarch over the whites and continue to beat until the whites are foamy. Raise the speed to high and very gradually add the sugar, beating until stiff, shiny peaks form. Quickly beat in the lemon juice and vanilla. Spread the meringue inside the circle drawn on the parchment, building up the edges slightly to form a rim.

Bake until the meringue is crispy, about 40 minutes. Turn off the oven and open the door. When the meringue is completely cool, remove it from the oven. Remove the parchment paper from the meringue and place the meringue on a serving plate.

In a clean bowl, using the electric mixer, beat the cream on medium-high speed until soft peaks form. Spoon the lemon curd into the hollow of the meringue, then spoon some of the whipped cream over the curd. Top with the strawberries and dust with confectioners' sugar (if using).

Cut the meringue into wedges and serve, passing the remaining whipped cream at the table.

FOR THE LEMON CURD

3 large eggs plus 3 large egg yolks

½ cup (4 oz/125 g) sugar

¼ cup (½ oz/15 g) grated or minced Meyer lemon zest

½ cup (125 ml) fresh Meyer lemon juice

¼ tsp salt

4 tbsp (2 oz/60 g) unsalted butter, cut into cubes and slightly softened

4 large egg whites

1 tbsp cornstarch

1 cup (8 oz/250 g) sugar

1 tsp fresh Meyer lemon juice

1 tsp pure vanilla extract

1 cup (250 ml) heavy cream

3 cups (12 oz/375 g) fresh strawberries, hulled and sliced or coarsely chopped if large

Confectioners' sugar, for dusting (optional)

serves 6–8

Kiwi & Passion Fruit Panna Cotta

A muffin pan is the ideal receptacle in which to nestle six glasses at an angle for chilling the primary layer of this lovely two-tone dessert. A ripe passion fruit will have slightly wrinkled skin and be either yellow or purple, depending on the variety.

FOR THE PANNA COTTA

1 tbsp (1 package) unflavored gelatin

1 cup (250 ml) whole milk

½ cup (4 oz/125 g) granulated sugar

1 cup (250 ml) very cold heavy cream

½ tsp vanilla bean paste or vanilla extract

FOR THE GELÉE

1 tbsp (1 package) unflavored gelatin

6 kiwifruits, about 1 lb (500 g) total, peeled and coarsely chopped

1–3 tsp superfine sugar (optional)

3 ripe passion fruits

serves 6

To make the panna cotta, in a small bowl, sprinkle the gelatin over 3 tbsp cold water. Let stand until softened, about 5 minutes. In a small saucepan, combine the milk and granulated sugar. Place over medium-low heat and heat, stirring occasionally, until the sugar is dissolved. Raise the heat to medium-high and bring just to a boil. Remove from the heat and let cool for 2 minutes. Stir in the gelatin until completely dissolved, then stir in the cream and vanilla. Pour ⅓ cup (80 ml) of the mixture into each of 6 small, stemless wineglasses or narrow juice glasses. Place each glass at a slight angle in one cup of a muffin pan and refrigerate until set, about 1½ hours.

Meanwhile, make the gelée: In a small bowl, sprinkle the gelatin over 3 tbsp cold water. Let stand until softened, about 5 minutes. In a food processor, purée the kiwifruits until very smooth. Measure the juice; you should have 2 cups (500 ml). If there is less, add water to reach 2 cups (500 ml) total; if there is more, reserve additional juice for another use. Pour half of the kiwi juice into a small saucepan. Place over high heat and bring just to a simmer, then remove from the heat. Stir in the gelatin until smooth, then stir in the remaining kiwi juice. Taste for sweetness and stir in a little superfine sugar, if needed. Let cool before topping the panna cotta; the gelée should be neither warm nor cold (if too cold, it will begin to set).

When the panna cotta layer is set (the top will jiggle slightly, which is okay) and the gelée is at room temperature, set the glasses upright and carefully pour ⅓ cup (80 ml) of the gelée on top of the angled panna cotta layer in each glass. Refrigerate the glasses upright until the gelée is set, at least 2 hours or up to overnight (if refrigerating overnight, cover with plastic wrap).

Cut the passion fruits in half. Scoop the flesh of one half atop each panna cotta and serve.

Rhubarb-Ginger Crumble with Cardamom Cream

Stalks of pink, red, or pale green rhubarb start to appear in markets and farm stands in late March. Although botanically a vegetable, this hardy plant usually turns up on dessert menus, in crisps and compotes, pies and tarts, and more.

Preheat the oven to 350°F (180°C). Lightly butter a shallow 2-qt (2-l) baking dish.

In a medium bowl, stir together the flour and brown sugar. Scatter 4 tbsp (2 oz/ 60 g) of the butter over the top and, using your fingers, 2 knives, or a pastry blender, work in the butter until the mixture is crumbly. Add the almonds, crystallized ginger, and salt and toss to combine. Set aside.

In a large bowl, combine the rhubarb, fresh ginger, and granulated sugar and toss to mix well. Transfer the rhubarb mixture to the prepared baking dish and spread in an even layer. Dot with the remaining 2 tbsp butter. Sprinkle the almond mixture evenly over the fruit. Bake until the topping is deep gold and the juices are bubbling, about 1 hour.

Meanwhile, make the cardamom cream: In a bowl, using an electric mixer, beat the cream, confectioners' sugar, cardamom, and vanilla on medium-high speed until soft peaks form. Refrigerate until ready to serve.

Serve the crumble with the cardamom cream.

6 tbsp (3 oz/90 g) unsalted butter, cut into ¼-inch (6-mm) cubes, plus more for greasing

1 cup (5 oz/155 g) all-purpose flour

¾ cup (6 oz/185 g) firmly packed golden brown sugar

¾ cup (4 oz/125 g) chopped almonds

⅓ cup (2 oz/60 g) finely chopped crystallized ginger

¼ tsp salt

2 lb (1 kg) rhubarb, trimmed and cut into ¾-inch (2-cm) pieces (about 6 cups/940 g)

1 tbsp peeled and minced fresh ginger

¾ cup (6 oz/185 g) granulated sugar

FOR THE CARDAMOM CREAM

1 cup (250 ml) heavy cream

1 tbsp confectioners' sugar

½ tsp ground cardamom

½ tsp pure vanilla extract

serves 6–8

Naked Carrot Cake with Spring Blossoms

When carrot cake is at its moist and flavorful best, the frosting can be kept to a bare (quite literally!) minimum. Cover the cake sides with just a thin sweep of frosting, leaving the layers exposed, then finish with a crown of edible spring blossoms.

Unsalted butter for greasing

3⅓ cups (17 oz/530 g) all-purpose flour, plus more for dusting

2¼ cups (1 lb/500 g) firmly packed golden brown sugar

1½ tbsp baking powder

1½ tsp ground cinnamon

¾ tsp salt

2¼ cups (11 oz/345 g) grated carrots

1 cup (250 ml) vegetable oil

6 large eggs, at room temperature

2 tsp pure vanilla extract

FOR THE FROSTING

½ lb (250 g) cream cheese, at room temperature

¾ cup (6 oz/185 g) unsalted butter, at room temperature

2 tsp pure vanilla extract

4 cups (1 lb/500 g) confectioners' sugar

Edible spring blossoms for garnish

serves 12–14

Preheat the oven to 325°F (165°C). Butter three 8-inch (20-cm) cake pans. Cut parchment paper to fit the bottoms of the pans and line the bottoms. Butter the parchment, then flour the parchment and pan sides.

In a large bowl, stir together the flour, brown sugar, baking powder, cinnamon, and salt. In a medium bowl, stir together the carrots, vegetable oil, eggs, and vanilla until blended. Stir the carrot mixture into the flour mixture until just blended.

Divide the batter among the prepared cake pans. Bake until a toothpick inserted into the center of a cake comes out clean, 25–27 minutes. Let cool in the pans on wire racks for 5 minutes, then remove the cakes from the pans and let cool completely on the racks. The cakes can be wrapped in plastic wrap and refrigerated for up to 3 days. Frost and decorate on the day you serve it.

To make the frosting, in a large bowl, using an electric mixer fitted with the paddle attachment, beat the cream cheese, butter, and vanilla on medium speed until smooth, about 2 minutes. Stop the mixer and scrape down the sides of the bowl with a rubber spatula. With the mixer on low speed, gradually beat in half of the confectioners' sugar until incorporated, then beat in the remaining confectioners' sugar until smooth. Use right away, or cover and refrigerate for up to 2 days.

To assemble, evenly slice off a thin layer from the rounded top of each cake to make it level, if necessary. Place a cake layer, bottom side down, on a serving plate. Top with about 1 cup (250 ml) frosting, spreading it evenly. Place another cake layer over the frosting, top with 1 cup (250 ml) frosting, and spread evenly. Add the third cake layer, bottom side up, and spread 1 cup (250 ml) frosting on top. Using an offset icing spatula or other straight-edged knife, spread the remaining frosting in a single sheer layer over the cake sides so that each layer is exposed. Garnish the top with edible blossoms, cut the cake into wedges, and serve.

DESSERT FOR ALL OCCASIONS
This towering carrot cake—its layers anchored with rich, creamy frosting—can cap off any springtime get-together, from a birthday party or Easter lunch to a Sunday dinner. Garnish with any edible blossoms in season. Try violets, redbud flowers, clover, dandelion, forsythia, wood sorrel, or pansies.

A Toast for Every Season

Pea + Radish

4 oz (125 g) goat cheese

4–8 sugar snap peas, blanched

2 small radishes, julienned

Fresh pea shoots

Spread the goat cheese evenly over the toasts.
Top with sugar snap peas, radishes, and pea shoots.

Tomato + Basil

4 oz (125 g) fresh mozzarella, sliced

1 cup (6 oz/180 g) cherry tomatoes, halved

Fresh basil and tarragon leaves

Arrange the mozzarella slices evenly over
the toasts. Top with the cherry tomatoes
and a sprinkling of fresh herbs.

These simple toasts are an ideal light lunch with soup or first course for a weekend supper. Toast slices of coarse country bread or whole-grain bread in a toaster or on a grill until golden and crisp, then finish with one of these seasonal toppings.

Mushroom + Sage

4 oz (125 g) teleme cheese

Leaves from 2 sprigs fresh sage

1 cup (3 oz/90 g) sliced mushrooms

2 tbsp unsalted butter

Spread the teleme evenly over the toasts. Sauté the mushrooms and sage leaves in butter until the mushrooms are soft, then spoon over the toasts.

Pomegranate + Walnut

4 oz (125 g) Stilton or blue cheese

¼ cup (1 oz/30 g) pomegranate seeds

¼ cup (1 oz/30 g) toasted, chopped walnuts

Leaves from 1 sprig rosemary

Spread the stilton evenly over the toasts. Top with pomegranate seeds, walnuts, and rosemary.

SUMMER

Color imbues kitchens in the summer months, with brilliant tomatoes, peppers, squashes, corn, stone fruits, melons, and berries all vying for their spot on the table. Grilled dishes and salads are favored now, as are the season's signature fruit pies and tarts.

FINISH WITH SALT
Choose any naturally
colored salt—Hawaiian
red or black, Himalayan
or Peruvian pink,
Persian blue—for
finishing this vegetarian
take on ceviche.

Summer Vegetable Ceviche

Here, I have treated some of summer's vegetable bounty—cucumber, zucchini, bell pepper—to the bright citrus and chile flavors of traditional ceviche. The addition of diced avocado adds a creamy richness.

Trim the ends from the cucumber, cut lengthwise into wedges, and trim away the seeds. Cut the wedges lengthwise into ¼-inch (6-mm) slices, then cut crosswise into ¼-inch (6-mm) dice.

In a large nonreactive bowl, whisk together the lime juice, orange juice, salt, red pepper flakes, and hot pepper sauce. Add the cucumber, jicama, orange and yellow bell peppers, zucchini, green onions, and pickled peppers and toss gently. Cover and refrigerate for 1–2 hours, tossing once or twice.

To serve, gently but thoroughly fold the avocados into the vegetables and divide among the lettuce leaves. Drizzle each with about ½ tsp citrus olive oil and a pinch of Hawaiian salt and serve.

½ **English cucumber, unpeeled**

½ **cup (125 ml) fresh lime juice**

¼ **cup (60 ml) fresh orange juice**

¾ **tsp salt**

Pinch of red pepper flakes

3 dashes of hot pepper sauce such as Tabasco

½ **small jicama, about 6 oz (185 g), peeled and finely diced**

1 small orange bell pepper, seeded and finely diced

1 small yellow bell pepper, seeded and finely diced

1 zucchini, trimmed and finely diced

6 green onions, white and pale green parts, thinly sliced

6 pickled peppers, such as Peppadew, finely chopped

2 small avocados, pitted, peeled, and diced

6 large or 12 small romaine lettuce leaves

Citrus-infused extra-virgin olive oil, preferably lemon, for drizzling

Hawaiian red or black sea salt or other colored sea salt for sprinkling

serves 6

Peach Flatbread with Burrata, Arugula & Pickled Onion

When you eat juicy peaches out of hand at the height of summer, putting them on flatbread is likely the furthest thing from your mind. But I encourage you to try this sunny topping of sweet yellow peaches, fresh green herbs, and creamy burrata.

1 ball Thin-Crust Dough (page 166), at room temperature

FOR THE PICKLED ONION

½ cup (125 ml) red wine vinegar or apple cider vinegar

½ cup (125 ml) dry red wine

¼ cup (60 g) sugar

¼ tsp red pepper flakes

1 tbsp kosher salt

½ small red onion, thinly sliced into rings

20 fresh basil leaves, torn into small pieces

½ cup (½ oz/15 g) loosely packed baby arugula leaves

1 tbsp extra-virgin olive oil, plus more for brushing

Fine sea salt and freshly ground black pepper

3 small ripe peaches, peeled, pitted, sliced, and diced

8 oz (250 g) burrata, pulled apart into small chunks

serves 6–12

Prepare the dough. Cover with a kitchen towel and set aside.

To make the pickled onion, in a small saucepan, combine the vinegar, wine, sugar, peppercorns, pepper flakes, and salt. Stir over low heat until the sugar and salt are dissolved. Add the onion slices and bring the liquid to a boil over high heat. Reduce the heat to medium-low and simmer until slightly softened, about 5 minutes. Let cool. Transfer the onion and all the liquid to a clean jar, cover tightly, and refrigerate for at least 2 hours or up to 1 week.

Preheat the oven to 550°F (290°C) and place a rack in the lower third of the oven. Lightly oil a rimmed baking sheet. Place the dough on the baking sheet and firmly press down in the center, then push and stretch the dough from the center to the pan edge, pressing gently with your fingertips, to achieve an even thickness into all four corners. If the dough springs back and is difficult to work with, cover and set aside for 10 minutes to relax, then continue to press the dough to the pan edges. Cover with a kitchen towel and let rise for 15 minutes. Make several dimples in the dough with your knuckles.

In a bowl, toss the basil and arugula with the olive oil and ¼ tsp salt.

Lightly brush the risen dough with olive oil. Scatter the peaches evenly over the top. Squeeze as much liquid as possible from the pickled onion, then scatter the slices evenly over the peaches. Season lightly with salt and pepper. Bake until the edges are golden brown, 12–14 minutes.

Remove the flatbread from the oven, dot the burrata chunks evenly over the top, then spoon over the basil and arugula mixture. Cut into pieces and serve.

Fried Squash Blossoms with Ricotta

Squash blossoms appear in late spring when zucchini plants begin to bloom, but continue through summer and even into fall. Each blossom has a mellow floral flavor and makes the perfect receptacle for a cheese filling.

Preheat the oven to 200°F (95°C).

In a bowl, stir together the cheese, basil, and parsley and season to taste with salt and pepper. Transfer to a pastry bag fitted with a large plain tip. Remove the stamens from the squash blossoms. Pipe about 1 tbsp of the cheese mixture into each blossom.

Place the flour in a shallow bowl. In another shallow bowl, beat the eggs until blended. Roll the squash blossoms in the flour, then in the eggs, and then in the flour again, shaking off the excess. Place on a plate.

In a large, deep frying pan, pour in the oil to a depth of 2 inches (5 cm) and heat over medium-high heat to 375°F (190°C) on a deep-frying thermometer. Working in batches, add a few blossoms to the oil at a time and fry, turning once, until golden, 3–4 minutes. Transfer the fried blossoms to a paper towel–lined plate and keep warm in the oven until all are fried. Allow the oil to return to 375°F (190°C) before frying the next batch. Serve warm.

1 cup (8 oz/250 g) whole-milk ricotta cheese

1 tbsp chopped fresh basil

½ tbsp chopped fresh flat-leaf parsley

Salt and freshly ground pepper

8–12 squash blossoms

All-purpose flour for dredging

2 large eggs

Canola oil for frying

serves 4–6

Heirloom Tomato Tart

Colorful heirloom tomatoes make any dish memorable, and this tart showcases them superbly. Tucked into a crisp crust over basil-studded corn kernels and two cheeses, the tomatoes bake until juicy and tender, retaining their sun-kissed flavor.

FOR THE CRUST

1½ cups (7½ oz/235 g) all-purpose flour

½ cup (2½ oz/75 g) cornmeal

1 tsp sugar

1¼ tsp salt

½ cup (4 oz/125 g) cold unsalted butter, cut into cubes

⅓ cup (80 ml) plus 1 tbsp ice water

3 tbsp olive oil

2 lb (1 kg) regular and cherry heirloom tomatoes

1 tbsp olive oil

4 green onions, thinly sliced

2 cloves garlic, minced

1 ear corn, husk and silk removed, and kernels cut off the cob

1 tbsp thinly sliced fresh basil, plus basil leaves for garnish

Salt and freshly ground pepper

2 oz (60 g) Gruyère cheese, shredded

2 tbsp grated Parmesan cheese

1 large egg yolk whisked with 1 tbsp whole milk

serves 4–6

To make the crust, in a food processor, combine the flour, cornmeal, sugar, and salt and pulse briefly to mix. Scatter the butter over the top and pulse just until evenly distributed but large chunks of butter remain visible. In a measuring cup, whisk together the ice water and olive oil. Gradually add the ice-water mixture to the flour mixture, pulsing just until the dough begins to hold together but small chunks of butter are still visible. Turn the dough out onto a piece of plastic wrap and press into a rough 4-by-8-inch (10-by-20-cm) rectangle. Cover with the plastic wrap and refrigerate until well chilled, at least 1 hour or up to 1 day.

Preheat the oven to 375°F (190°C).

Core the regular tomatoes and cut crosswise into thick slices about ⅓ inch (9 mm) thick. Cut cherry tomatoes in half. Place the slices in a single layer on several layers of paper towels, cover with another paper towel, and let drain.

Meanwhile, in a frying pan, warm the olive oil over medium-low heat. Add the green onions and garlic and cook, stirring occasionally, until softened, about 2 minutes. Add the corn kernels and cook, stirring occasionally, for 30 seconds. Remove from the heat, stir in the basil, and season to taste with salt and pepper. Let cool.

Place a 15-inch (38-cm) square of parchment paper on a work surface. Transfer the dough to the parchment and roll out into a 9-by-14-inch (23-by-35-cm) rectangle. Slide the parchment with the dough onto a baking sheet. Spread the corn mixture over the dough, leaving a 2-inch (5-cm) uncovered border. Sprinkle the Gruyère and Parmesan evenly over the corn. Arrange the tomato slices in an even layer over the cheeses. Lift the edges of the dough and fold them over the filling, leaving the center uncovered. Brush the edges of the dough with the egg mixture.

Bake until the crust is golden and the tomato juices are bubbling, 35–40 minutes. Scatter basil leaves over the tart, cut into slices, and serve warm.

Blistered Padrón Peppers with Spicy Garlic Aioli

Padrón peppers are at their best in the heat of summer and need little more than a sprinkling of flaky sea salt and a squeeze of lemon to enjoy them. The aioli is an added benefit, adding a creamy, lightly spiced finish to the peppers' mellow heat.

FOR THE AIOLI

3 large egg yolks, at room temperature

2 cloves garlic, minced

Kosher salt

Generous pinch of cayenne pepper

1 cup (250 ml) extra-virgin olive oil

2 tbsp fresh lemon juice

1 lb (500 g) Padrón peppers

1 lemon, quartered

1 tbsp olive oil

Flaky sea salt, such as Maldon

serves 4

To make the aioli, combine the egg yolks, garlic, 1 tsp salt, and cayenne pepper in a food processor. Process until all ingredients are combined, about 30 seconds. With the motor running, very slowly drizzle in olive oil to form a thick emulsion, drizzling faster as the mixture thickens. Add the lemon juice, process until well combined, and transfer the aioli to a small serving bowl. Set aside.

Prepare a grill for direct-heat cooking over high heat or preheat a stove-top grill pan over high heat.

In a large bowl, toss the peppers and quartered lemon with the olive oil. Grill the peppers and lemon, turning with tongs, until the skins of the peppers are blistered on all sides and the lemon wedges are nicely charred, 3–4 minutes. Season the peppers with sea salt and serve with the lemon and aioli.

Golden Gazpacho with Torn Croutons & Cherry Tomato Salsa

With the bright yellow soup as a backdrop, the red cherry tomato salsa here offers an extra splash of color. Croutons are a classic accompaniment to gazpacho and add welcome crunch and a bit of buttery flavor to the mix.

In a food processor, pulse the bell peppers, cucumber, tomatoes, and onion to a coarse purée. Transfer the contents of the food processor to a large bowl. Add the garlic, vinegar, and olive oil and stir to combine. Season to taste with salt, pepper, and hot pepper sauce. Refrigerate until well chilled, at least 1 hour.

To make the croutons, preheat the oven to 400°F (200°C). Place the bread on a baking sheet. Drizzle the butter over the bread, season with salt and pepper, and toss to coat evenly. Bake until golden and crisp, 10–15 minutes. Let cool.

To make the salsa, in a small bowl, stir together the cherry tomatoes, serrano chile, green onion, garlic, cilantro, and lime juice. Set aside until ready to serve.

Ladle the gazpacho into bowls, garnish with the croutons and a spoonful of the salsa, and serve.

2 yellow bell peppers, seeded and chopped

1 English cucumber, peeled, seeded, and chopped

4 yellow tomatoes, about 2 lb (1 kg) total, chopped, with all their juices

1 small yellow onion, chopped

2 cloves garlic, minced

2 tbsp white wine vinegar

¼ cup (60 ml) extra-virgin olive oil

Salt and freshly ground pepper

Hot pepper sauce such as Tabasco

FOR THE TORN CROUTONS

¼ lb (125 g) day-old sourdough bread, crusts removed and bread torn into small pieces

3 tbsp unsalted butter, melted

Salt and freshly ground pepper

FOR THE SALSA

1 pint (12 oz/375 g) mixed cherry tomatoes, quartered

1 serrano chile, seeded and minced

1 green onion, thinly sliced

1 small clove garlic, minced

1 tbsp chopped fresh cilantro

Juice of ½ lime

serves 6–8

SEEK SEASONAL VARIETY
Summer is the season for cucumbers. Lemon or English cucumbers work well in this recipe, as do mild, crisp Persian or Armenian cucumbers.

Thai Beef Salad with Cucumber, Chile & Greens

Salads, with their cool, fresh flavors, are a summer-menu mainstay. This recipe brings together staples of the season: crisp cucumbers—either lemon or other mild variety—hot chile, sweet bell pepper, and a mix of herbs.

To make the vinaigrette, in a large bowl, whisk together the fish sauce, lime juice, sugar, and chile. Set aside.

Prepare a grill for direct-heat cooking over high heat and oil the grill rack, or preheat the broiler.

Sprinkle the flank steak evenly with salt and pepper and rub the seasonings into the meat. Brush lightly on both sides with 2 tsp grapeseed oil. Grill the steak directly over the heat, or place on a broiler pan and broil, turning once, until seared on the outside and cooked rare to medium-rare in the center, about 4 minutes on each side. Transfer the steak to a cutting board, tent with aluminum foil, and let rest for 20 minutes.

Cut the steak across the grain on the diagonal into very thin slices. Add the slices to the bowl with the vinaigrette and toss to coat. Add the lettuce, cucumber, onion, bell pepper, mint, cilantro, and basil. Toss until well mixed and serve.

FOR THE VINAIGRETTE

3 tbsp Thai fish sauce

3 tbsp fresh lime juice

2 tsp sugar

1–2 tsp minced fresh hot chile with seeds

Grapeseed or canola oil for greasing and brushing

1 small flank steak, flatiron steak, or skirt steak, ¾–1 lb (375–500 g)

Salt and freshly ground pepper

1 large head butter or other soft-textured leaf lettuce, torn into bite-size pieces

1 cup (5 oz/155 g) thinly sliced lemon or English cucumber and cut into half moons

½ cup (2 oz/60 g) thinly sliced red onion

½ cup (2½ oz/75 g) red bell pepper strips

½ cup (¾ oz/20 g) lightly packed fresh mint leaves

½ cup (¾ oz/20 g) lightly packed torn fresh cilantro leaves

¼ cup (⅓ oz/10 g) lightly packed torn fresh basil leaves, preferably Thai

makes 4 servings

Farro, Grilled Corn & Summer Squash Salad

The nutty flavor and slightly chewy texture of Italian farro is an ideal partner to summer produce. Both the grilled corn and squash take on a slight smoky flavor here. You can use semipearled or pearled farro, but allow extra time to make it.

1 cup (7 oz/220 g) quick-cooking farro

6 tbsp (3 oz/90 g) unsalted butter, melted

3 drops hot pepper sauce such as Tabasco, or small pinch of cayenne pepper

2 tbsp finely chopped fresh basil

Salt and freshly ground pepper

6 ears white or yellow corn, husks and silk removed

2 small yellow squash, cut lengthwise into slices about ⅓ inch (9 mm) thick

2 small zucchini, cut lengthwise into slices about ⅓ inch (9 mm) thick

Extra-virgin olive oil for brushing

½ cup (¾ oz/20 g) coarsely chopped fresh flat-leaf parsley

FOR THE DRESSING

3 tbsp fresh lemon juice

2 tsp Dijon mustard

3 cloves garlic, minced

Salt and freshly ground pepper

⅔ cup (160 ml) extra-virgin olive oil

serves 6

Prepare the farro according to the package directions. Drain well and set aside.

In a bowl, whisk together the butter, hot pepper sauce, basil, ½ tsp salt, and ¼ tsp pepper. Have ready 3 sheets of aluminum foil. Place 2 ears of corn on each sheet and brush each pair with one-third of the butter mixture. Wrap the aluminum foil around each pair of corn, forming a total of 3 packages.

Prepare a grill for direct-heat cooking over medium-high heat, or preheat a grill pan on the stovetop over medium-high heat. Grill the foil-wrapped corn, turning occasionally, for 10 minutes. Unwrap the corn, place the ears directly on the grill rack or pan, and grill, turning as needed, until evenly charred, 5–10 minutes longer. Watch carefully: The corn should be nicely charred but not blackened. Set aside.

Brush the squash and zucchini slices lightly on both sides with olive oil, and season with salt and pepper. Grill until slightly charred and tender-crisp, 2–4 minutes on each side.

When the corn is cool enough to handle, cut the corn kernels from the cobs and transfer to a serving bowl. Dice the squash and zucchini slices and add to the corn. Add the farro and the parsley and toss to mix.

To make the dressing, in a large bowl, whisk together the lemon juice, mustard, garlic, ½ tsp salt, and ¼ tsp pepper. Whisking constantly, slowly add the olive oil and whisk until well combined.

Drizzle the dressing over the salad, toss until well mixed, and serve.

Risotto with Fresh Corn & Basil Oil

With luck, your local corn season stretches from early summer into fall, allowing you to enjoy this simple, satisfying risotto a few times each year. Any variety of corn will do, though choosing a bicolored variety creates a particularly attractive dish.

In a large saucepan, melt the butter over medium heat. Add the leeks and stir to coat. Reduce the heat to medium-low, cover, and cook until translucent, about 5 minutes.

Meanwhile, in a medium saucepan, combine the broth and 3 cups (750 ml) water. Place over medium heat and warm the broth mixture, adjusting the heat to keep the mixture hot but not simmering. Raise the heat under the leeks to medium, add the rice, and cook, stirring, until the rice is translucent, about 3 minutes. Begin adding the broth mixture ½ cup (125 ml) at a time, stirring constantly and adding more liquid only when the previous addition has been absorbed.

Meanwhile, cut the corn kernels from the cobs. After about 10 minutes of stirring and adding liquid to the rice as needed, stir in the corn. It should take about 20 minutes for the rice to absorb all of the liquid and become al dente and creamy. If you need more liquid, use boiling water. Season to taste with salt and pepper.

Remove the risotto from the heat and stir in the chives and 2 tbsp of the basil olive oil. Divide among bowls, top with the remaining 2 tbsp basil oil, and serve.

2 tbsp unsalted butter

1 cup (3 oz/90 g) thinly sliced leeks, white and pale green parts, or 1 small yellow onion, finely chopped

2 cups (500 ml) chicken broth

1½ cups (10½ oz/330 g) short-grain rice, such as Arborio, Carnaroli, or Vialone Nano

2–3 ears corn, husks and silk removed

Salt and freshly ground pepper

2 tbsp finely snipped fresh chives

4 tbsp (60 ml) basil-infused extra-virgin olive oil

serves 4

Rice-Noodle Salad with Chicken, Summer Vegetables & Herbs

A spiralizer is the ideal tool for cutting vegetables like zucchini, cucumber, and carrot into long thin strips for this salad. Cellophane (bean-thread) or udon noodles can be used for the rice noodles; prepare them according to the package directions.

6 bone-in, skin-on chicken thighs, about 2¼ lb (1.1 kg) total

Olive oil for brushing

1 tsp ground cumin

Salt and freshly ground pepper

FOR THE VINAIGRETTE

3 tbsp rice vinegar

2 tbsp fresh lime juice

2 tbsp fish sauce

1 tbsp soy sauce

1 tbsp toasted sesame oil

1 tsp sugar

½–1 tsp Sriracha or other hot sauce, or to taste

3 cloves garlic, minced

½ lb (250 g) thin dried rice noodles

½ English cucumber

1 large carrot, peeled

1 small zucchini

1 yellow bell pepper, seeded and cut into ¼-inch (6-mm) julienne

10 green onions, white and pale green parts, thinly sliced

⅓ cup (½ oz/15 g) small fresh basil leaves

¼ cup (⅓ oz/10 g) fresh mint leaves

serves 6

Preheat the oven to 375°F (190°C). Set a flat wire rack inside a small roasting pan.

Pat the chicken thighs dry with paper towels. Brush the chicken lightly on both sides with olive oil, sprinkle with the cumin, and season generously with salt and pepper. Place on the rack in the roasting pan and roast, turning once, until golden brown and opaque at the center, or a meat thermometer inserted into the center registers 160°F (71°C), 25–30 minutes. Let cool.

To make the vinaigrette, in a large bowl, whisk together the vinegar, lime juice, fish sauce, soy sauce, sesame oil, sugar, Sriracha, and garlic until well combined. Set aside.

Bring a large saucepan of water to a boil over high heat, then remove from the heat. Add the rice noodles and let stand, stirring occasionally, until just tender, 3–5 minutes. Drain, rinse well with running cold water, and shake the colander well. (Or prepare according to the package directions.) Add the noodles to the bowl with the vinaigrette and toss to coat.

Pull the chicken meat from the bones and shred it, keeping the skin intact if desired. Add half of the chicken to the bowl with the noodles, reserving the remaining chicken for serving. Using a spiralizer, mandoline, or julienne peeler, cut the cucumber, carrot, and zucchini into julienne strips and add to the bowl. Add the yellow pepper and toss gently to mix.

Divide the salad among 6 plates and top with the remaining chicken and the green onions. Sprinkle with the basil and mint and serve.

PICNIC FARE

Pack this easy-to-transport salad in a cooler along with some cold beer and ginger ale and tote it to your favorite summer picnic spot.

Stone Fruit Salad with Summer Lettuces, Hazelnuts & Goat Cheese

Lettuces are traditionally cool-weather crops, but some varieties thrive in summer heat, keeping salad greens on July and August menus. Every lettuce type—Bibb, crisphead, romaine, looseleaf—includes heat-tolerant varieties.

FOR THE VINAIGRETTE

2 tbsp rice vinegar

1 tsp honey

Salt and freshly ground pepper

½ cup (125 ml) extra-virgin olive oil

6 cups (¾ lb/375 g) lightly packed mixed summer lettuces

2 firm but ripe small plums, halved, pitted, and thinly sliced

2 firm but ripe small apricots, halved, pitted, and thinly sliced

1 firm but ripe peach, halved, pitted, and thinly sliced

¼ cup (1½ oz/45 g) hazelnuts, toasted, skinned, and coarsely chopped

¼ cup (1½ oz/45 g) crumbled firm goat cheese

serves 6

To make the vinaigrette, in a small bowl, whisk together the vinegar, honey, and a pinch each of salt and pepper. Whisking constantly, slowly add the olive oil and whisk until well combined.

Put the lettuces in a large bowl, drizzle with some of the vinaigrette, and toss to coat. Scatter the plums, apricots, peach, and hazelnuts over the lettuce, drizzle with the remaining vinaigrette, and toss gently to mix. Sprinkle with the cheese and serve.

Watermelon, Nectarine & Mint Salad with Feta Cheese

The appeal of this easy salad is its delightful crunch and cool temperature—perfect for the dog days of summer. Keep the watermelon in the fridge until just before serving, then work quickly to assemble the salad on chilled plates.

Chill 6 salad plates.

In a small saucepan, bring the vinegar to a simmer over medium heat, swirling occasionally, until thickened to the consistency of maple syrup, 10–12 minutes. Remove from the heat. (The balsamic syrup can be made weeks in advance and refrigerated; warm it gently just until fluid before using.)

In a large, shallow bowl, gently fold together the watermelon, nectarines, cheese, and half of the mint. Divide the salad among the chilled plates and drizzle with the balsamic syrup and pistachio oil. Sprinkle with the pistachios and the remaining mint and serve.

⅓ cup (80 ml) balsamic vinegar

2 lb (1 kg) seedless watermelon, rind removed, flesh cut into ¾-inch (2-cm) cubes

4 ripe nectarines, about 1¼ lb (600 g) total, halved, pitted, and sliced

6 oz (185 g) mild feta cheese, cut into ½-inch (12-mm) dice

3 tbsp finely chopped fresh mint

1½ tbsp pistachio oil

¼ cup (1 oz/30 g) coarsely chopped unsalted pistachios

serves 6

GRILL KNOW-HOW

A boneless rib eye, a top candidate for backyard barbecues, turns out best— more tender and flavorful—when grilled medium-rare.

Grilled Rib-Eye Steak with Avocado Chimichurri

These days, I find it more appealing to serve steak sliced rather than whole. One large rib eye generally serves two, so adjust the number of steaks you buy based on their size and the appetites of your diners.

In a food processor, combine the parsley, oregano, garlic, olive oil, 1½ tsp salt, and 1 tsp black pepper and process until chopped but still a little chunky. Alternatively, chop the ingredients by hand. Transfer the mixture to a bowl and stir in the red pepper flakes. Set aside, or cover and refrigerate for up to 3 hours.

Prepare a grill for direct-heat cooking over high heat, or preheat a grill pan on the stovetop over high heat.

Brush the steaks on both sides with olive oil and season generously with salt. Grill the steaks over the hottest part of the fire for 2½ minutes, moving them after the first minute only if the fire flares up. Turn and sear on the second side for 2½ minutes longer. Move the steaks to a cooler part of the grill (or reduce the heat) and continue to grill, turning several times to brown evenly, until an instant-read thermometer inserted into the thickest part of the steaks registers 130°–135°F (54°–57°C) for medium-rare, about 8 minutes longer. Season the steaks generously with black pepper. Transfer to a carving board, tent with aluminum foil, and let rest for 4–5 minutes.

Just before serving, finish the chimichurri by stirring the avocado and vinegar into the parsley mixture. Cut the steaks crosswise into slices about ¼ inch (6 mm) thick.

Divide the steak slices among warmed individual plates, top each with a generous spoonful of the chimichurri, and serve.

1½ cups (1½ oz/45 g) firmly packed fresh flat-leaf parsley leaves and tender stems

3 tbsp lightly packed fresh oregano leaves

6 cloves garlic, minced

¾ cup (180 ml) extra-virgin olive oil, plus more for brushing

Salt and freshly ground black pepper

⅛–¼ tsp red pepper flakes

4 well-marbled boneless rib-eye steaks or New York strip steaks, each about 1 lb (250 g) and 1½ inches (4 cm) thick, at room temperature

1 large or 2 small avocados, pitted, peeled, and diced

2 tbsp white wine vinegar

serves 6–8

Grilled Salmon with Stone Fruit–Herb Mojo

I have three rules for grilling fish: have the fish very cold, have the grill very hot, and avoid sticking by lightly coating the fish with mayonnaise. Make the mojo no more than 2 hours ahead, or the citrus will discolor the herbs.

FOR THE MOJO

3 tbsp extra-virgin olive oil

Grated zest of 1 small orange

Grated zest of 1 small lemon

Grated zest of 1 small lime

2 tbsp fresh orange juice

2 tsp fresh lemon juice

2 tsp fresh lime juice

3 cloves garlic, minced

1 large shallot, finely chopped

Salt and freshly ground pepper

2 large ripe nectarines or peaches, or 4 plums, halved, pitted, and finely diced

2 tbsp finely chopped fresh flat-leaf parsley

2 tbsp finely snipped fresh chives

1 tbsp mayonnaise

1 tsp extra-virgin olive oil

4 center-cut skin-on salmon fillets, 6–8 oz (185–250 g) each and about 1 inch (2.5 cm) thick, very cold

Salt and freshly ground pepper

serves 4

To make the mojo, in a bowl, whisk together the olive oil, citrus zests and juices, garlic, shallot, ½ tsp salt, and ¼ tsp pepper. Add the nectarines, parsley, and chives and stir gently to mix. Set aside. (The mojo can be covered and refrigerated for up to 2 hours; bring to room temperature before serving.)

Prepare a grill for direct-heat cooking over high heat.

In a small bowl, stir together the mayonnaise and olive oil. Brush the fish fillets on both sides with the mayonnaise mixture and season with salt and pepper. Grill the fillets, skin side down and without moving them, until a wide metal spatula slipped under the fillets can lift them off the grill rack without too much sticking, 6–8 minutes. Gently turn the fish over and continue to grill until the outer flesh is opaque but the center is still a little translucent, 2–4 minutes longer, or until done to your liking.

Transfer the fish to a platter, removing any charred skin. Spoon a generous amount of the mojo over the fish and serve.

Zucchini Lasagna with Herbed Ricotta & Fresh Heirloom Tomato Sauce

In my career as a recipe developer, I have made "lasagna" out of everything from potatoes and polenta to wonton wrappers. This version, which calls for ribbons of zucchini in place of the traditional noodles, is by far the prettiest and the lightest.

Make the tomato sauce and set aside.

To make the filling, in a bowl, use a fork to thoroughly whisk together all the filling ingredients. Let stand at room temperature while you grill the zucchini.

Preapre a grill for direct-heat cooking over medium heat, or preheat a grill pan on the stove top over high heat. In a large baking dish, toss the zucchini slices with the olive oil, ½ teaspoon salt, ¼ teaspoon pepper, and the oregano. Grill the zucchini in batches until tender and grill-marked, 1–3 minutes per side.

Assemble the lasagna: Preheat the oven to 375°F (190°C). Using ¾ cup (180 ml) of the tomato sauce, make an even layer in a 6-by-11-inch (15-by-28-cm) baking dish, and top with a layer of grilled zucchini. Using 1¼ cups (300 g) of the ricotta mixture, dollop the mixture over the zucchini and spread it evenly. Add another layer of zucchini, another layer of ricotta, and a final layer of zucchini. Spoon remaining tomato sauce over the top and bake uncovered for 25 minutes. Distribute the mozzarella over the top and bake for 10 minutes more, until the mozzarella is melted but not browned. Switch the oven to broil and broil until the mozzarella is nicely blistered. Remove from the oven and let rest for 10 minutes to set. Cut into squares and serve, garnished with basil blossoms if desired.

1 recipe Tomato Sauce
(page 167)

FOR THE FILLING

12 oz (375 g) whole-milk ricotta, at room temperature

6 oz (180 g) feta cheese, crumbled

3 green onions, minced

1 tbsp finely chopped fresh flat-leaf parsley, chervil, or tarragon

1 tbsp finely chopped fresh basil

¼ tsp fine sea salt

¼ tsp ground pepper

¼ tsp ground nutmeg

2 large eggs, lightly beaten

1½–1¾ lb (750-875 g) green zucchini, ends trimmed, cut lengthwise into ¼-inch (6-mm) slices

2–3 tbsp olive oil

Fine sea salt and freshly ground pepper

1 tsp dried Greek oregano

5 oz (150 g) fresh mozzarella, sliced and torn into large pieces

Basil blossoms, for garnish (optional)

serves 6

STRAWBERRIES

BLUEBERRIES

PLUMS

BLACKBERRIES

NECTARINES

PEACHES

Summer Fruits

Summertime markets are
flooded with freshly picked
stone fruits and berries in
a wild mix of varieties.
Select peaches, nectarines,
apricots, plums, and cherries
that are plump, free of
bruises, give only slightly
to pressure, and have good
color and a vivid aroma.
Pick out berries—blueberries,
strawberries, raspberries,
blackberries, boysenberries—
that are sweet, succulent,
richly colored, and fragrant,
then handle them gently and
use them within a day or two.

Grilled Fish Tacos with Pineapple Salsa & Avocado Crema

You can change up the ingredients in this colorful, health-savvy salsa, depending on what looks best at the market. For example, mango or melon can replace the pineapple, and a yellow or orange bell pepper can stand in for the red one.

FOR THE PINEAPPLE SALSA

1 small pineapple, about 2 lb (1 kg), peeled, cored, and diced

½ *each* red onion, finely chopped, and red bell pepper, seeded and finely chopped

1 small English cucumber, peeled, seeded, and diced

½ jalapeño chile, seeded and finely chopped

½ cup (¾ oz/20 g) chopped fresh cilantro

2 tbsp fresh lime juice

2 tbsp extra-virgin olive oil

Salt and freshly ground pepper

FOR THE AVOCADO CREMA

1 avocado

1 cup (8 oz/250 g) crema or plain yogurt

2 tsp fresh lime juice

¾ tsp ground cumin

Salt

1 tbsp vegetable oil

1 lb (500 g) boneless, skinless snapper or other mild, firm whitefish fillets

Salt and freshly ground pepper

8 small corn tortillas, 6 inches (15 cm) in diameter

1 lime, cut into wedges

serves 4

To make the pineapple salsa, in a large bowl, toss together the pineapple, onion, bell pepper, cucumber, jalapeño, and cilantro. Add the lime juice and olive oil, season with salt and pepper, and stir to mix well. Cover and refrigerate until ready to serve.

To make the avocado crema, halve and pit the avocado and scoop the flesh into a food processor. Add the crema, lime juice, cumin, and ¼ tsp salt and process just until smooth. Transfer the crema to a bowl, cover, and refrigerate until ready to serve.

Prepare a grill for direct-heat cooking over medium-high heat.

Drizzle the vegetable oil over the fish fillets, rub to coat evenly, and season with salt and pepper. Grill the fish over the hottest part of the fire, carefully turning once with a wide spatula, until opaque and nicely charred, 6–8 minutes total. Transfer the fish to a platter, break into 8 pieces, and tent with aluminum foil.

Working in batches, grill the tortillas, turning once or twice, until warmed through, 1–2 minutes.

To assemble the tacos, place 2 tortillas on each serving plate and top with a piece of fish, a spoonful of the pineapple salsa, and a drizzle of the crema. Pass the lime wedges and any remaining salsa and crema at the table.

AT THE FISH COUNTER
Choose whitefish that is sustainably caught or farmed, such as wild or farmed bass, wild Pacific halibut, or farmed tilapia.

Grilled Pork Chops with Summer Plums & Thyme

Nowadays, pork is bred to be lean, so to ensure a flavorful, succulent result here, purchase thick chops and don't stint on the brining time. Once the pork has been brined and the grill has been fired up, this dish comes together quickly.

FOR THE BRINE

¼ cup (60 ml) cider vinegar

¼ cup (2 oz/60 g) firmly packed golden brown sugar

1 tsp dried thyme

1 tsp juniper berries (optional)

⅛ tsp red pepper flakes

2 tbsp salt

1 tbsp freshly ground black pepper

6 bone-in pork loin chops, about 6 oz (180 g) each and at least 1 inch (2.5 cm) thick

Canola oil for brushing

6 slightly firm but ripe plums, halved and pitted

6 fresh thyme sprigs

serves 6

To make the brine, in a large bowl, combine 6 cups (1.5 l) water, the vinegar, brown sugar, thyme, juniper berries (if using), red pepper flakes, salt, and black pepper and stir until the sugar and salt are dissolved.

Place the pork chops in a large lock-top plastic bag and pour in the brine. Seal the bag closed, massage the brine around the chops, and refrigerate overnight.

At least 30 minutes before you plan to begin grilling, remove the chops from the brine; discard the brine. Rinse the chops briefly in cold water and pat dry with paper towels.

Prepare a grill for indirect-heat cooking over medium heat; the temperature inside the grill should be 350°–375°F (180°–190°C). If using charcoal, bank the lit coals on either side of the grill bed, leaving a strip in the center without heat. If using gas, preheat the burners, then turn off one or more of the burners to create a cooler zone. Brush and oil the grill rack.

Place the pork chops on the grill directly over the heat and sear, turning once, until nicely grill-marked on both sides, 2–3 minutes on each side. Move the chops to the indirect-heat area, cover the grill, and cook until the chops are somewhat firm to the touch, about 15 minutes for medium, or until an instant-read thermometer inserted horizontally into the center of a chop, away from the bone, registers 145°F (63°C). Transfer the chops to a platter and let rest for 10 minutes.

Meanwhile, brush both sides of the plum halves with canola oil, place directly over the heat, and grill until nicely grill-marked, about 2 minutes on each side. Transfer the plums to the platter with the pork chops. Pull the leaves from the thyme sprigs, sprinkle evenly over the chops and plums, and serve.

Pounded Chicken Breasts with Grilled Ratatouille

Ratatouille is the iconic summertime dish of Provence. In this nontraditional version, the vegetables are cooked on a grill until just tender and infused with a slightly smoky taste, and then the dish is finished on the stove top.

One at a time, place the chicken breasts between two pieces of plastic wrap. Lightly pound with a meat pounder, starting from the centers and working towards the sides, to an even thickness of about ⅜ inch (1 cm).

In a large baking dish, whisk together 1½ tbsp of the olive oil, the vinegar, oregano, anchovy paste (if using), ¼ tsp salt (if using anchovy paste; ¾ tsp salt if not using anchovy paste), and ⅛ tsp black pepper. Add the chicken and turn to coat both sides. Refrigerate, uncovered, for 30–40 minutes while you prepare the ratatouille.

Prepare a grill for direct-heat cooking over medium-high heat.

Brush the bell peppers, onion, zucchini, eggplant, and tomatoes lightly on both sides with olive oil and season with salt and black pepper. Working in batches if necessary, grill the peppers, onion, zucchini, and eggplant directly over the heat, turning occasionally, until nicely grill-marked, 3–7 minutes on each side (the peppers will take the longest). Do not overcook. As the vegetables are done, transfer them to a cutting board. Grill the tomatoes, cut sides down, directly over the heat until shriveled, about 3 minutes. Pull off and discard the skins and set the tomatoes aside. Cut the other grilled vegetables into a small dice.

In a large sauté pan, combine the remaining 3 tbsp olive oil, the tomato paste, garlic, thyme, red pepper flakes, ¼ tsp salt, and ¼ tsp black pepper. Place over medium-high heat and, when the oil is warm and the garlic has just begun to sizzle, add the tomatoes, mashing them to blend with the aromatic ingredients. Cook until the tomatoes have broken down, about 3 minutes. Add the grilled diced vegetables and stir gently to combine. Cover, reduce the heat to medium-low, and cook, stirring occasionally, until the mixture is just slightly softened and saucy, 8–10 minutes. Season to taste with salt and black pepper.

Grill the chicken breasts until firm and golden, 1½–2 minutes on each side. Transfer to a serving platter. Fold 2 tbsp of the basil into the ratatouille and spoon over the chicken. Sprinkle with the remaining 2 tbsp basil and serve.

4 boneless, skinless chicken breasts, about 1¼ lb (625 g) total

4½ tbsp olive oil, plus more for brushing

1 tbsp white wine vinegar

½ tsp finely chopped fresh oregano

½ tsp anchovy paste (optional)

Salt and freshly ground black pepper

1 large or 2 small red or yellow bell peppers, seeded and quartered lengthwise

1 small white or yellow onion, cut crosswise into ⅓-inch (8 mm) rings

2 zucchini, cut lengthwise into ¼-inch (6-mm) slices

1 Asian eggplant, halved crosswise and cut lengthwise into ¼-inch (6-mm) slices

2 plum tomatoes, cored, halved crosswise, and seeded

4 tsp tomato paste

4 cloves garlic, minced

¼ tsp dried thyme

⅛ tsp red pepper flakes

4 tbsp (⅓ oz/10 g) slivered fresh basil

serves 4–6

Blackberry & Blueberry Potpies

At the height of summer, blackberries and blueberries are plump, juicy, and sweet—perfect for a pie filling. If you can't find blackberries, use boysenberries or olallieberries, while sweet-tart huckleberries can replace the blueberries.

Prepare the dough and refrigerate as directed.

Preheat the oven to 375°F (190°C). Line a baking sheet with parchment paper.

In a large saucepan, combine the blackberries, blueberries, granulated sugar, lemon zest and juice, cardamom, and salt. Place over medium heat and cook, stirring occasionally, until some of the berries begin to burst and the liquid reduces slightly, 5–7 minutes. Remove from the heat and gently stir in the cornstarch. Let cool.

On a lightly floured work surface, roll out the dough into a round about ⅛ inch (3 mm) thick. Cut out 4 rounds of dough, each about ½ inch (12 mm) larger than the diameter of the ramekins. Cut a vent or two into each dough round. Divide the berry filling evenly among four 1-cup (250-ml) ramekins and dot with the butter. Brush the rim of each ramekin with some of the egg mixture, place a dough round on top, and press the edges down over the rim to secure. Brush the dough rounds with the egg mixture and sprinkle with turbinado sugar, if using.

Place the ramekins on the prepared baking sheet and bake until the crust is golden and the berry juices are bubbling, 35–40 minutes. Let cool for about 10 minutes. Serve each potpie topped with a scoop of vanilla ice cream.

1 recipe Flaky Pie Dough (page 166)

2 cups (8 oz/250 g) blackberries

2 cups (8 oz/250 g) blueberries

¾ cup (6 oz/185 g) granulated sugar

½ tsp grated lemon zest

1 tbsp fresh lemon juice

¼ tsp ground cardamom

Pinch of salt

2 tbsp cornstarch

All-purpose flour for dusting

1 tbsp unsalted butter, diced

1 large egg beaten with 1 tsp water

Turbinado sugar for sprinkling (optional)

Vanilla ice cream for serving

serves 4

Apricot Pistachio Tart

The apricot season is fleeting, with the first fruits appearing in markets in late spring and the last disappearing by the beginning of August, so buy them when you see them or you will miss out on this memorable tart.

All-purpose flour for dusting

1 sheet frozen all-butter puff pastry, thawed according to package directions

10 apricots (about ¾ lb/350 g), halved and pitted

2 tbsp sugar

1 tbsp orange liqueur

½ cup (5 oz/155 g) thick apricot preserves

1 tsp ground cinnamon

½ tsp ground cardamom

6 tbsp (1½ oz/45 g) chopped unsalted pistachios

2 tbsp honey

serves 8

Preheat the oven to 400°F (200°C).

On a lightly floured surface, roll out the puff pastry sheet into an 11-inch (28-cm) square and transfer to a 10-inch (25-cm) square tart pan with a removable bottom. Trim off the corners, then gather any dough overhang and press it into the sides of the pan to form a rim that is even in thickness. Using a fork, prick the bottom and sides of the dough. Freeze the tart shell for 15 minutes. Bake until lightly golden, about 15 minutes. Let cool on a wire rack for about 30 minutes.

Meanwhile, in a bowl, stir together the apricots, sugar, and orange liqueur. Let stand at room temperature for 15 minutes.

Spread the apricot preserves evenly over the bottom of the tart shell. Sprinkle the cinnamon, cardamom, and 4 tbsp (1 oz/30 g) of the pistachios over the preserves. Arrange the apricots, cut sides down, on top and drizzle with any juices remaining in the bowl. Sprinkle the remaining 2 tbsp pistachios over the top. Bake until the apricots are tender and the pastry is golden brown, 30–40 minutes.

Remove the tart from the oven and drizzle the honey over the top. Let cool on a wire rack for about 1 hour. (The tart can be baked up to 4 hours in advance and cooled, then tented with aluminum foil and stored at room temperature.)

When ready to serve, let the pan sides fall away, then slide the tart onto a serving plate. Cut into slices and serve.

Summer Cherry Clafoutis

This rustic dessert of central France tops fresh fruit with a custard-like batter and is then baked until the fruit is tender and the top is golden brown. Sweet, dark cherries are the traditional fruit, but plums or apricots would also be good.

Place a rack in the upper third of the oven and preheat to 350°F (180°C). Generously butter a shallow 1½-qt (1.5-l) baking dish.

Arrange the cherries in the prepared baking dish.

In a saucepan, combine the milk and cream. Place over medium-low heat and warm until small bubbles form around the edges. Remove from the heat and vigorously whisk in the flour, a little at a time, until no lumps remain.

In a bowl, whisk together the eggs, granulated sugar, and salt. Slowly whisk in the milk mixture and the almond extract to make a batter. Pour the batter over the cherries.

Place the dish on a baking sheet and bake until lightly browned, 45–55 minutes. Let cool on a wire rack for about 10 minutes. Dust with confectioners' sugar and serve warm.

Unsalted butter for greasing

1 lb (500 g) fresh dark sweet cherries, such as Bing, Regina, Black Tartarian, or Tulare, pitted

1 cup (250 ml) whole milk

¼ cup (60 ml) heavy cream

½ cup (1½ oz/45 g) sifted cake flour

4 large eggs, at room temperature

½ cup (4 oz/125 g) granulated sugar

⅛ tsp salt

½ tsp almond extract

Confectioners' sugar for dusting

serves 6

Watermelon Mojito Pops

At the end of a hot summer day—or in the middle of one—nothing revives quite as nicely as one of these Cuban-inspired fruity cocktail ice pops. Serve them to guests when they arrive for a barbecue, or enjoy one when you need a pick-me-up.

½ small watermelon, about 2 lb (1 kg)

5 tbsp (2½ oz/70 g) superfine sugar

4 tbsp (60 ml) white rum

4 tbsp (60 ml) fresh lime juice, plus ½ tsp minced lime zest

2 tbsp chopped fresh mint

makes six 3-oz (90-g) ice pops

Scoop the flesh from the watermelon and remove any seeds. Reserve the rind. Chop the watermelon flesh; you should have about 3½ cups (18 oz/510 g). Transfer the watermelon flesh to a blender or food processor. Add 3 tbsp of the sugar, 3 tbsp of the rum, and 2 tbsp of the lime juice and blend until smooth. Transfer to a large glass measuring cup and stir in the mint.

Divide the watermelon flesh mixture among 6 ice pop molds, filling them about four-fifths full. Freeze until partially frozen, about 1 hour.

Meanwhile, using a spoon, scrape away and discard any remaining watermelon flesh from the rind, then use a sharp knife to cut off the fibrous, dark green peel. Chop enough of the rind to measure about ¾ cup (about 4 oz/125 g). Transfer the chopped rind to a blender or food processor. Add the remaining 2 tbsp sugar, 1 tbsp rum, and 2 tbsp lime juice, and 2 tbsp water, plus the lime zest. Blend until smooth. Transfer to a large glass measuring cup.

Once the popsicles are beginning to harden, pour an equal amount of the rind mixture over each pop, filling the molds until full. Insert the popsicle sticks, cover, and freeze until solid, at least 3 hours or up to 3 days.

CHANGE THE SPIRIT

To switch from Cuban to Mexican pops, substitute tequila for the rum. Prefer the pops virgin? Skip the spirit.

A Galette for Every Season

Strawberry + Mint

1 cup (8 oz/250 g) Nutella

3 cups (14 oz/440 g) sliced strawberries

Fresh mint leaves and rosemary blossoms for garnish

Spread the Nutella evenly over the bottom of the baked tart shell. Layer the cut strawberries over the top. Sprinkle with the mint and blossoms.

Stone Fruit

½ cup (4 oz/125 g) peach jam

4 nectarines and/or peaches, pitted and sliced

3 plums, pitted and sliced

Fresh edible summer blossoms for garnish

Spread the jam evenly over the bottom of the baked tart shell. Layer the nectarines and/or peaches, and the plums, evenly over the top. Sprinkle with the blossoms.

A fruit galette goes together quickly with store–bought all–butter puff pastry. Thaw a ½-lb (250-g) pastry sheet, roll lightly just to flatten, score a line around the perimeter about ¾ inch (2 cm) from the edge, then prick the middle with a fork so it doesn't puff while baking. Bake in a preheated 375°F (190°C) oven until golden, then top with cut fruit and seasonal garnishes. Each recipe serves four.

Pear + Walnut

6 oz (180 g) Stilton cheese

4 ripe pears, cored and sliced

1 cup (4 oz/125 g) toasted chopped walnuts

Honey for drizzling

Crumble the Stilton evenly over the bottom of the baked tart shell. Layer the pears evenly over the top. Sprinkle with the walnuts. Drizzle liberally with honey.

Citrus

½ cup (4 oz/125 g) lemon curd (page 45) or lime curd

3 cups (1½ lb/750 g) sliced assorted citrus fruits, such as navel oranges, blood oranges, tangerines, and kumquats

Spread the curd evenly over the bottom of the baked tart shell. Layer the citrus slices evenly over the top.

FALL

As the days shorten and the nights cool, hard-skinned squashes, earthy mushrooms, and a wealth of brassicas—kale, chard, cauliflower, cabbage—make their way into braises and roasts, soups and stews. Apples and figs shine now too, in dishes both savory and sweet.

GO DOMESTIC
When wild mushrooms
are unavailable or beyond
your budget, choose
flavorful domesticated
varieties, such as shiitake,
cremini, king trumpet,
and oyster.

Creamy Parmesan Polenta with Wild Mushrooms

Enhanced with plenty of butter and good-quality Parmesan, creamy polenta makes a rich bed for a collection of the season's wild mushrooms. Select the best mushrooms you can find, leaving the prettiest ones whole for the topping.

In a saucepan, combine 8 cups (2 l) water and 1½ tsp salt. Bring to a boil over high heat. Slowly add the polenta, stirring constantly, then reduce the heat to low and cook, stirring often, until the polenta pulls away from the sides of the pan, about 40 minutes.

In a frying pan, melt 1 tbsp of the butter with the olive oil over medium-high heat. Add the shallot and mushrooms and cook, stirring occasionally, until the mushrooms are tender, 8–10 minutes. Season with salt and pepper. Keep warm until ready to serve.

When the polenta is done, stir in the remaining 3 tbsp butter, the cheese, 1 tsp salt, and 1 tsp pepper. Cook, stirring occasionally, until the butter and cheese have melted, 3–4 minutes.

Spoon the polenta into bowls and top with the mushrooms. Sprinkle with thyme, if using, and serve, passing additional cheese at the table.

Salt and freshly ground pepper

1½ cups (8 oz/250 g) polenta

4 tbsp (2 oz/60 g) unsalted butter

1 tbsp olive oil

1 tbsp minced shallot

1 lb (500 g) assorted wild mushrooms, such as chanterelles, porcini, morels, or lobster mushrooms, brushed clean and coarsely cut or left whole depending on size

½ cup (2 oz/60 g) grated Parmesan cheese, plus more for serving

Thyme leaves or chopped fresh flat-leaf parsley for garnish (optional)

serves 6–8

Fig, Blue Cheese & Walnut Crostini with Honey Drizzle

The flavors of plump, sweet figs and salty, pungent blue cheese complement each other nicely. Select fruits that give slightly to pressure and have a few tiny fissures in an otherwise smooth surface, signaling they are ripe and bursting with flavor.

8 fresh figs, stemmed and halved lengthwise

1 tbsp balsamic vinegar

Salt and freshly ground pepper

¼ cup (1 oz/30 g) chopped walnuts

½ cup (2½ oz/75 g) crumbled blue cheese

8 slices toasted ciabatta or whole-grain bread, each ½ inch (12 mm) thick

½ cup (½ oz/15 g) arugula leaves

2 tbsp honey

serves 8

Preheat the oven to 400°F (200°C). Line a baking sheet with parchment paper.

Place the figs, cut side up, on the prepared baking sheet. Drizzle with the vinegar and season with salt and pepper. Roast the figs until very tender, 10–15 minutes. Set aside.

Reduce the oven temperature to 350°F (180°C). Spread the walnuts on a piece of aluminum foil and toast until fragrant, about 5 minutes. Set aside.

Sprinkle a heaping 1 tbsp of the blue cheese over each slice of toasted bread. Top each with 2 fig halves, a sprinkling of walnuts and arugula leaves, and a drizzle of honey. Season lightly with salt and pepper and serve.

Smoky Eggplant Dip with Cumin-Crusted Pita Chips

Eggplant season typically runs from July through October, making this luscious dip an ideal autumn appetizer or snack. It gets its heady smoky flavor from the charred skin of the eggplant and its nutty richness from the tahini.

Preheat the oven to 400°F (200°C). Line a rimmed baking sheet with aluminum foil.

To make the pita chips, in a small frying pan, toast the cumin seeds over medium heat, stirring frequently, until fragrant, about 2 minutes. Pour onto a plate to cool. Transfer the cumin seeds to a spice mill or mortar, add the salt, and grind or crush with a pestle until finely ground.

Brush the pita breads on both sides with the olive oil, cut them into 8 wedges each, and arrange the wedges on the prepared baking sheet. Sprinkle the tops evenly with the cumin mixture. Bake until the wedges are light golden brown and crisp, 10–15 minutes, turning them over halfway through baking.

Meanwhile, begin making the eggplant dip: Trim off the stem ends of the garlic. Place the cloves on a small square of aluminum foil, drizzle with the 1 tsp olive oil, and wrap the cloves securely in the foil. Place on the pan with the pita chips and bake until the garlic is soft when tested with a small knife, about 15 minutes. Unwrap the garlic and let stand until cool enough to handle. Set the pita chips aside.

Preheat the broiler. Line a broiler pan with aluminum foil and lightly grease with olive oil. Place the eggplants, cut side down, on the prepared pan and broil until the skins char and the eggplant flesh is tender, about 20 minutes. Transfer the eggplant to a colander and set it in the sink to drain and cool slightly.

Using a spoon, scrape the eggplant flesh out of the skins into a blender. Squeeze the garlic from its skins and add to the blender along with the lemon juice, tahini, and a scant ¼ tsp salt. Blend the ingredients until smooth, and then season to taste with salt. Transfer the dip to a serving bowl and let stand for a few minutes to allow the flavors to blend.

Sprinkle the dip with the paprika and place on a platter. Arrange the pita chips alongside and serve.

FOR THE PITA CHIPS

1 tsp cumin seeds

¾ tsp kosher salt

3 pita breads, 7 inches (18 cm) in diameter

1½ tbsp olive oil

FOR THE DIP

6 cloves garlic, unpeeled

1 tsp olive oil, plus more for greasing

2 globe eggplants, about 2 lb (1 kg) total, halved lengthwise

2 tbsp fresh lemon juice

¼ cup (2½ oz/75 g) tahini

Salt

¼ tsp smoked paprika

serves 8

Wheat Berry Salad with Chopped Chard, Pear & Sunflower Seeds

This crisp salad highlights some of fall's signature flavors. The dusky, deep green leaves of the chard offer a nice visual contrast to the crimson of the chard stems and the soft white of the pears. Fuyu persimmons can also make a lovely addition.

¾ cup (5½ oz/170 g) wheat berries

Salt and freshly ground pepper

4 large red Swiss chard leaves

3 tbsp extra-virgin olive oil

2 tbsp walnut oil

4 green onions, thinly sliced

2 small pears, unpeeled, cored, and sliced

1½ tbsp sherry vinegar

¼ cup (1 oz/30 g) lightly toasted sunflower seeds or pepitas

serves 4–6

In a small saucepan, combine the wheat berries and 1¾ cups (430 ml) lightly salted water. Place over high heat and bring to a boil. Reduce the heat to medium-low, partially cover the pan, and simmer very gently until the wheat berries are tender but firm to the bite, 15–18 minutes. Remove from the heat, fluff with a fork, and let cool. (The wheat berries can be made ahead; cover and set aside at room temperature for up to 2 hours, or refrigerate for up to 6 hours.)

Separate the stems from the chard leaves by cutting along both sides of the center vein. Finely chop the stems. Sliver the leaves crosswise.

In a large bowl, combine the wheat berries, chard stems and leaves, olive oil, walnut oil, ½ tsp salt, and ¼ tsp pepper. Toss to mix well. Fold in the green onions and pears, drizzle with the vinegar, and gently toss again. Sprinkle with the sunflower seeds and serve.

EASY FLAVOR INFUSION
This simple vinaigrette, mixed directly in the salad bowl for ease, would also be good made with hazelnut, pistachio, or pecan oil.

Coconut-Curry Butternut Squash Soup

As the weather cools, this fragrant, spicy Thai-inspired soup is a welcome sight on the dinner table. If you like, trade in kabocha or calabaza squash for the butternut, as both have the same naturally sweet flavor.

1 large butternut squash, about 4 lb (2 kg)

1½ tbsp olive oil

4 large shallots, about 3 oz (90 g) total, sliced

1 tbsp peeled and grated fresh ginger

1 clove garlic, minced

3 cups (750 ml) chicken broth or vegetable broth, plus more as needed

Salt

1 tsp Thai red curry paste

¾ cup (180 ml) light coconut milk

Fresh lime juice, or to taste

serves 4–6

Using a sharp, heavy knife, trim the stem end from the squash, then cut in half lengthwise. Scoop out the seeds and discard. Peel the squash and then cut the flesh into 1-inch (2.5-cm) cubes. (You should have about 9 cups/3 lb/ 1.5 kg squash).

In a large pot, warm the olive oil over medium heat. Add the shallots and cook, stirring occasionally, until softened, 2–3 minutes. Add the ginger and garlic and cook, stirring occasionally, until fragrant but not browned, about 1 minute. Add the squash, broth, and ½ tsp salt and bring to a boil over high heat. Reduce the heat to medium-low, cover, and simmer until the squash is tender, about 20 minutes. Remove from the heat and let cool slightly.

In a small bowl, whisk together the curry paste and coconut milk until well blended. Set aside.

In a blender or food processor, working in batches if necessary, process the soup until smooth. Return the soup to the pot and stir in the coconut milk mixture plus more broth if needed to reach the desired consistency. Reheat the soup gently over medium heat until just hot. Season to taste with lime juice and salt. Ladle the soup into warmed bowls and serve.

Kale, White Bean & Sausage Soup

Hardy, earthy kale fills produce markets in the fall and winter, and any variety is delicious here. Its peppery flavor is complemented by smoky, spicy Polish kielbasa, though other smoked sausages work too. Serve crusty country bread with the soup.

In a large pot, warm the olive oil over medium-high heat. Add the onion and garlic and cook, stirring occasionally, until translucent, about 5 minutes. Stir in the kale, potato, kielbasa, and red pepper flakes and season generously with salt. Pour in 8 cups (2 l) water and bring to a boil over high heat. Reduce the heat to medium-low and simmer until the kale is almost tender, about 20 minutes.

Add the white beans and cook until heated through, about 5 minutes. Season to taste with salt and black pepper. Ladle the soup into warmed bowls and serve.

2 tsp olive oil

1 large yellow onion, chopped

4 cloves garlic, chopped

1 bunch kale, about ¾ lb (375 g), tough stems removed, leaves cut crosswise into ½-inch (12-mm) strips

1 Yukon gold potato, about ½ lb (250 g), cut into 1-inch (2.5-cm) pieces

2 oz (60 g) pork or turkey kielbasa sausage, sliced

⅛ tsp red pepper flakes

Salt and freshly ground black pepper

1 can (15 oz/470 g) white beans, drained and rinsed

serves 4

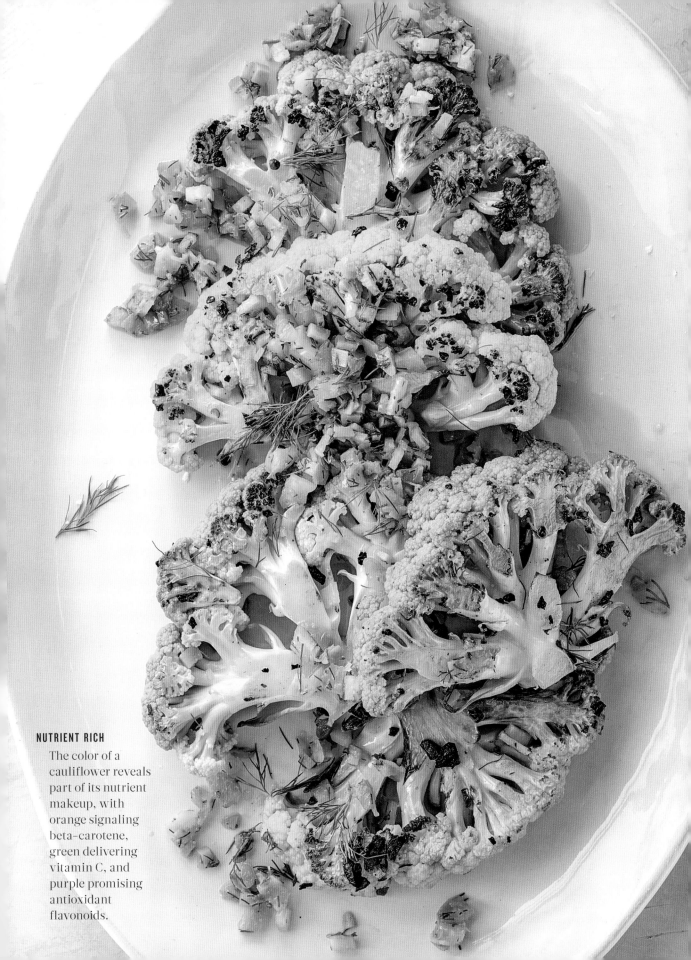

NUTRIENT RICH
The color of a cauliflower reveals part of its nutrient makeup, with orange signaling beta-carotene, green delivering vitamin C, and purple promising antioxidant flavonoids.

Seared Cauliflower Steaks with Olive-Caper Gremolata

It is difficult to cut more than two "steaks" from each head of cauliflower because each slice needs a substantial portion of the stem to hold it together. That means you will have a pile of stray florets from this recipe for adding to a curry, soup, or pasta.

To make the gremolata, in a bowl, stir together the celery, green onion, capers, olives, dill, and orange zest. Set aside.

Trim the base of 1 head of cauliflower, removing all the greens but keeping as much of the stem as possible intact. Using a large serrated knife, carefully slice the cauliflower through the middle of the stem to create 2 halves, then cut off the rounded outer parts of each half to create a total of 2 steaks, each about 1¼ inches (3 cm) thick and flat on both sides; reserve the crumbly outer florets for another use. Repeat with the second head of cauliflower.

In each of 2 large frying pans (preferably cast iron), warm 2 tbsp of the olive oil over medium-low heat. Divide the garlic and red pepper flakes between the pans, and season generously with salt and black pepper. Add 2 cauliflower steaks to each pan and cook without moving until golden brown, 4–5 minutes; maintain a low sizzle so the cauliflower doesn't scorch. Use a wide spatula, turn the steaks over and cook on the second sides until golden brown, 4–5 minutes longer. Remove the pans from the heat, cover, and let the cauliflower steaks steam for 5 minutes to help them soften; they should be tender when pierced with a skewer.

Transfer the cauliflower steaks to a serving platter, scatter with a generous amount of the gremolata, and serve.

FOR THE GREMOLATA

1 rib celery, finely chopped

1 green onion, white and pale green parts, finely chopped

2 tbsp capers, rinsed and finely chopped

4 large green olives, preferably Bella di Cerignola, pitted and finely chopped

1½ tbsp chopped fresh dill

Grated zest of 1 orange

2 small heads white, green, or orange cauliflower

4 tbsp olive oil

2 cloves garlic, smashed

⅛–¼ tsp red pepper flakes

Salt and freshly ground black pepper

serves 4

Romaine & Roasted Delicata Squash Salad with Dates, Almonds & Bacon

Fall is the season to celebrate hard-shelled cool-weather squashes in all their glorious hues and flavors. With its edible skin, the Delicata is particularly attractive in this salad, while the dates offer sweetness and the nuts add texture.

1 large Delicata squash, about 1 lb (500 g)

1 tbsp extra-virgin olive oil

Salt and freshly ground pepper

FOR THE VINAIGRETTE

6 slices thick-cut bacon

6 tbsp (90 ml) extra-virgin olive oil

2 tbsp balsamic vinegar

1½ tsp whole-grain mustard

1 shallot, minced

2 small cloves garlic, minced

Salt and freshly ground pepper

2 hearts romaine lettuce, cut crosswise into 1-inch (2.5-cm) pieces

6 pitted dates, halved lengthwise, then sliced crosswise

⅔ cup (2½ oz/75 g) sliced raw almonds

serves 4–6

Preheat the oven to 500°F (260°C).

Cut the squash in half lengthwise and then again crosswise. Scoop out and discard the seeds, then cut each quarter into ½-inch (12-mm) wedges. Place the squash in a small roasting pan, toss with the olive oil, and season generously with salt and pepper. Roast until tender but not mushy, 12–14 minutes, tossing every 5 minutes. Set aside.

To make the bacon vinaigrette, in a frying pan, cook the bacon over medium-low heat, turning as needed, until crisp and brown, about 4 minutes total. Drain on paper towels, then break apart into large pieces.

In a large bowl, whisk together the olive oil, vinegar, mustard, shallot, garlic, ½ tsp salt, and ¼ tsp pepper until well combined. Add the romaine and toss to coat. Gently fold in the squash, dates, bacon, and half of the almonds. Sprinkle with the remaining almonds and serve.

Soft Tacos with Pumpkin, Black Beans & Avocado

Roasting accentuates the mellow sweetness of Sugar pumpkins—one of the best varieties for cooking. Paired with cumin-spiced black beans, fresh corn, and sliced avocado, these fully loaded vegetarian tacos make an ample meal.

Preheat the oven to 425°F (220°C).

Arrange the pumpkin in a single layer on a rimmed baking sheet, drizzle with 2 tbsp of the olive oil, and toss gently to coat. Sprinkle with the chili powder and season with salt and pepper. Roast, stirring once halfway through, until the pumpkin is tender, about 30 minutes.

In a frying pan, warm the remaining 1 tbsp olive oil over medium heat. Add the onion and cook, stirring often, until very tender, about 5 minutes. Add the garlic and cook, stirring often, for 1 minute. Add the cumin, black beans, and corn and stir until heated through, about 1 minute.

To serve, fill each tortilla with some of the pumpkin, bean mixture, avocado, cheese, and cilantro, then finish with a squeeze of lime.

1 small Sugar pumpkin or butternut squash, about 1¾ lb (875 g), peeled, seeded, and cut into ½-inch (12-mm) cubes

3 tbsp olive oil

⅛ tsp chili powder

Salt and freshly ground pepper

½ small yellow onion, finely chopped

1 clove garlic, minced

½ tsp ground cumin

1 can (14½ oz/455 g) black beans, drained and rinsed

1 ear corn, husk and silk removed and kernels cut from the cob

12 corn or flour tortillas, 6–7 inches (15–18 cm) in diameter, warmed

1 avocado, pitted, peeled, and sliced

1 cup (5 oz/155 g) crumbled cotija or feta cheese

½ cup (½ oz/15 g) fresh cilantro leaves

1 or 2 limes, cut into wedges

serves 4–6

Pappardelle with Romanesco & Kalamata Olives

Despite its name, Romanesco broccoli is actually more closely related to cauliflower than broccoli. Whatever its lineage, I often prefer this showy chartreuse head of spiral florets over both of its kin because its florets don't crumble when cut apart.

FOR THE GARLICKY BREAD CRUMBS

1½ tbsp olive oil

3 small cloves garlic, minced

4 anchovy fillets in olive oil, drained on a paper towel

¼ tsp red pepper flakes

⅔ cup (1 oz/30 g) panko bread crumbs

Grated zest of 1 lemon

⅓ cup (½ oz/15 g) coarsely chopped fresh flat-leaf parsley

2 small or 1 large head Romanesco broccoli, about 1½ lb (750 g) total, tough ends trimmed

⅓ cup (80 ml) olive oil

Salt and freshly ground black pepper

36 large Kalamata olives, pitted and coarsely chopped

1 lb (500 g) pappardelle or fettuccine

serves 4–6

To make the bread crumbs, in a small frying pan, warm the olive oil over low heat. Add the garlic, anchovies, and red pepper flakes and cook, stirring, to begin breaking down the anchovies, 4–5 minutes. Raise the heat to medium-high, add the panko, and cook, stirring constantly, until golden brown, 3–4 minutes. Remove from the heat and stir in the lemon zest and parsley. Set aside.

In a steamer basket set over a large saucepan of simmering water, steam the whole head(s) of Romanesco until just slightly softened, about 5 minutes. Transfer to a cutting board and, when cool enough to handle, trim off the small green florets; discard the stem.

In a large sauté pan, warm the olive oil over medium-high heat. Add the florets, season with salt and black pepper, and cook, shaking the pan frequently, until golden brown, about 6 minutes. Stir in the olives and remove from the heat.

Meanwhile, bring a large pot of generously salted water to a boil over high heat. Add the pasta and cook until al dente, about 10 minutes, or according to the package directions. Drain well, reserving ⅓ cup (80 ml) of the cooking water. Add the pasta to the pan with the Romanesco, then add the reserved cooking water and toss to coat the pasta. Fold in three-fourths of the bread crumbs until well combined. Season to taste with salt and black pepper.

Transfer the pasta to a warmed platter or individual plates. Scatter the remaining bread crumbs on top and serve.

EASY ADAPTABILITY
Cauliflower—in any color—can step in here, as can wide ribbon pastas, such as tagliatelle and fettuccine, and short cuts, such as penne and fusilli.

PERFECT THE AUTUMN LUNCH
Precede the salad with your go-to black bean soup, set out a rustic walnut levain, and finish with Roasted Figs with Mascarpone (page 119).

Turmeric-Spiced Shrimp with Red Cabbage & Carrot Slaw

Here, garlicky, turmeric-dusted shrimp are complemented by a citrusy slaw that showcases two regulars of the fall market, red cabbage and carrots. Don't use shelf-weary turmeric, as it will lack its prized earthy flavor and saffron-like color.

To make the slaw, in a large bowl, whisk together the orange juice, vinegar, grapeseed oil, garlic, Tabasco, cumin, ½ tsp salt, and ¼ tsp pepper until well combined. Add the cabbage, carrots, onion, and half each of the cilantro and orange zest and stir until combined. Cover and refrigerate for at least 1 hour or up to 2 hours so the vegetables wilt slightly and the flavors marry.

In a wide, shallow bowl, stir together the flour, turmeric, chile powder, and ½ tsp salt. Add the shrimp and toss to coat lightly but evenly.

In a large frying pan, warm the grapeseed oil over medium-high heat (use 2 smaller pans if needed to prevent crowding). Add the garlic and cook, stirring continuously, until golden brown, 45–60 seconds. Using a slotted spoon, remove and discard the garlic.

Return the pan to medium heat. Add the butter and, when the foam subsides, add half the shrimp in a single layer and cook for 1 minute, then turn and continue to cook until pink and firm, 1–2 minutes longer. (You will need to start turning the shrimp that were added first as soon as you add the last one; keep track of the order so you don't overcook them.) Transfer the shrimp to a platter and keep warm while you cook the remaining shrimp.

Serve the shrimp with the slaw on the side, sprinkled with the remaining cilantro and orange zest.

FOR THE SLAW

½ cup (125 ml) fresh orange juice, plus grated zest of 2 large oranges

3 tbsp white-wine vinegar

¾ cup (180 ml) grapeseed or canola oil

2 cloves garlic, minced

½ tsp Tabasco or other hot pepper sauce

½ tsp ground cumin

Salt and freshly ground pepper

2 cups (6 oz/185 g) slivered red cabbage

2 large carrots, peeled and julienned, shaved, or spiralized

¼ cup (¾ oz/20 g) finely chopped red onion

3 tbsp finely chopped fresh cilantro

¼ cup (1 oz/30 g) superfine or all-purpose flour

1 tsp ground turmeric

½ tsp chili powder

Salt

1½ lb (750 g) jumbo shrimp, peeled and deveined, tails intact if desired

2 tbsp grapeseed or canola oil

4 cloves garlic, smashed

1 tbsp unsalted butter

serves 6

Chicken Tagine with Roasted Squash, Haricots Verts, Chickpeas & Cranberries

The term *tagine* refers both to the conical earthenware vessel in which this North African braise is traditionally cooked and to the dish itself. If you don't have haricots verts, regular green beans, which must cook a bit longer, will do in a pinch.

1 small acorn squash, about 1¼ lb (625 g), halved, seeded, and cut into ¾-inch (2-cm) chunks

3 tbsp olive oil

Salt and freshly ground pepper

2 lb (1 kg) boneless, skinless chicken thighs, trimmed and cut into 1-inch (2.5-cm) pieces

1 large yellow onion, finely chopped

¾ tsp ground cumin

½ tsp ground turmeric

4 cloves garlic, minced

2 cups (500 ml) chicken broth

2 bay leaves

1 cinnamon stick

1 can (15 oz/470 g) chickpeas, drained and rinsed

About 3 oz (90 g) haricots verts or green beans, trimmed and cut on the diagonal into ¾-inch (2-cm) lengths

⅔ cup (2½ oz/75 g) fresh or thawed frozen cranberries

Cooked couscous or rice, warm and buttered, for serving

¼ cup (1 oz/30 g) sliced raw almonds

2 tbsp coarsely chopped fresh flat-leaf parsley or cilantro

Grated zest of 1 lemon

serves 4–6

Preheat the oven to 500°F (260°C).

Place the squash in a roasting pan, toss with 1 tbsp of the olive oil, and season generously with salt and pepper. Roast until tender but not mushy, 13–15 minutes, stirring every 5 minutes. Set aside.

Meanwhile, season the chicken generously with salt and pepper. In a heavy cast-iron casserole or Dutch oven, warm the remaining 2 tbsp olive oil over medium-high heat. Add the chicken and cook, turning with tongs, until browned on all sides, about 12 minutes. Transfer the chicken to a platter.

Add the onion to the pot and cook, stirring frequently, until softened and slightly golden, 5–7 minutes. Add the cumin, turmeric, and garlic and cook, stirring frequently, for 1 minute. Return the chicken to the pot and add the broth, bay leaves, cinnamon stick, ¾ tsp salt, and plenty of pepper. Cover and cook over the lowest possible heat—just so the liquid simmers—until the flavors have melded and the chicken is tender, about 1 hour. Check occasionally; if the liquid level falls too low, add 1–2 tbsp water.

Trnasfer the chicken to the platter and tent with aluminum foil. Remove and discard the bay leaves and cinnamon stick. Add the chickpeas and haricots verts to the pot, raise the heat to medium-high, and simmer briskly until the juices are reduced and the beans are tender-crisp, 5–6 minutes. Return the chicken to the pot and stir to combine. Gently fold in the roasted squash and the cranberries, cover, and cook without stirring until the cranberries pop, 2–3 minutes. Remove from the heat and season to taste with salt and pepper.

Spoon the warmed couscous onto a platter. Spoon the chicken, vegetables, and sauce over the top. Garnish with the almonds, parsley, and lemon zest and serve.

Turkey Breast with Chanterelle Ragout

Long ago, I learned the trick of draping a "butter blanket" over a roasting turkey to ensure a shiny, mahogany skin, a technique that works equally well with a turkey breast. The added step of brining the breast will banish any talk of dry turkey.

Select a deep, nonreactive 4-qt (4-l) container—large enough to hold the turkey and brine but still fit inside your refrigerator. Pour 8 cups (2 l) cold water into the container. Set aside. In a small saucepan, combine the salt, sugar, and 2 cups (500 ml) water. Place over low heat and stir just until the salt and sugar are dissolved, then remove from the heat and let cool. Add to the cold water in the container along with the bay leaves and turkey breast, making sure the turkey is completely submerged. Refrigerate for at least 48 hours or up to 72 hours.

About 3 hours before serving time, remove the turkey from the brine, rinse under cold running water, and pat thoroughly dry with paper towels; discard the brine. Lift the skin from the breast and season the meat underneath with the thyme and plenty of pepper. Replace the skin and place the breast, skin side up, on a rack in a roasting pan. Season the skin generously with pepper. Cover the turkey loosely with a kitchen towel and let stand at room temperature for 1 hour.

Preheat the oven to 400°F (200°C). In a small saucepan, combine the butter, wine, and ¼ tsp pepper. Place over low heat and heat, stirring occasionally, until the butter melts. Remove from the heat. Unfold a piece of cheesecloth that's as long as the turkey breast, then refold it into a 4-layer square to cover the turkey from edge to edge and top to bottom. Dip the cheesecloth into the butter mixture to thoroughly saturate. Remove the towel from the turkey, then drape with the cheesecloth, covering the turkey completely.

Roast the turkey for 20 minutes, then reduce the oven temperature to 325°F (165°C). Continue to roast, basting occasionally with the pan juices, until an instant-read thermometer inserted into the thickest part of the meat registers 150°F (65°C), 2–2½ hours.

When the turkey is almost done, make the ragout.

Transfer the turkey to a carving board and let rest for 4–6 minutes. Remove the cheesecloth and cut the turkey crosswise into slices ½ inch (12 mm) thick. Arrange on warmed plates, top with the ragout, and serve the remaining ragout at the table.

½ cup (4 oz/125 g) kosher salt

¼ cup (2 oz/60 g) sugar

2 bay leaves

1 boneless turkey breast,
8–9 lb (4–4.5 kg),
any netting removed

½ tsp dried thyme

Freshly ground pepper

6 tbsp (3 oz/90 g) salted butter

⅓ cup (80 ml) fortified or
dessert wine, such as
Madeira, sherry, Marsala,
or orange muscat

1 recipe Chanterelle Ragout
(page 167)

serves 6–8

Pork Skewers with Apple, Fresh Sage & Rustic Bread

The Fuji—sweet, crisp, colorful—is a good choice here, but other red-skinned good-size fall varieties, such as Gala, Empire, Honeycrisp, Macoun, or Winesap, would also shine in this weeknight main course.

1 pork tenderloin, about 1 lb (500 g), silverskin removed and trimmed of excess fat

2 slices bacon, each cut crosswise into 8 pieces

⅓ cup (80 ml) olive oil

Grated zest and juice of 1 lemon

2 cloves garlic, minced

2 tsp plus 1 tbsp finely chopped fresh flat-leaf parsley

½ tsp smoked paprika

¾ tsp salt

¼ tsp freshly ground pepper

16 cubes (1-inch/2.5-cm cubes) rustic bread

16 fresh sage leaves

1 crisp red-skinned apple, such as Fuji

Lemon wedges for serving (optional)

serves 4

If using wooden skewers, soak 8 skewers in water to cover for at least 1 hour, then drain.

Cut the pork tenderloin into 1-inch (2.5-cm) cubes. You will need 16 cubes. Reserve any remaining pork for another use.

In a large bowl, combine the pork, bacon, olive oil, lemon zest and juice, garlic, 2 tsp of the parsley, the paprika, salt, and pepper. Add the bread cubes and sage and toss to coat the bread thoroughly. Let stand, tossing once or twice, for about 15 minutes.

Meanwhile, core the apple and cut into 8 wedges. Cut each wedge crosswise into 3 pieces to yield a total of 24. Add to the bowl and toss; the bread should be thoroughly coated with the flavored oil. If not, toss again.

Preheat the broiler. Line a baking sheet with aluminum foil.

Onto each skewer, thread an apple piece, pork cube, folded-over sage leaf, and bacon piece, then repeat the sequence, ending with a third apple piece. Use all of the ingredients to make a total of 8 skewers.

Place the skewers on the prepared baking sheet and broil, turning once, until the pork is nicely browned on the outside but still slightly pink inside and the bread is golden brown, 6–8 minutes total. When turning the skewers, use tongs and a spatula to prevent the pieces of food from rotating.

Transfer the skewers to plates and sprinkle with the 1 tbsp parsley. Serve with lemon wedges, if you like.

HEAD OUTDOORS
If your fall weather is warm enough to fire up the grill, move these skewers outdoors, using about the same timing.

Short Ribs with Carrot-Apple Purée

Some home cooks shy away from short ribs because they take a bit of time to cook. But long, slow, moist cooking breaks down their collagen (protein) to yield perfectly tender, juicy meat that is definitely worth the time investment.

5 lb (2.5 kg) bone-in beef short ribs, cut 2 inches (5 cm) thick, excess fat trimmed

Salt and freshly ground pepper

1 tsp ground fennel (optional)

2 tbsp olive oil

2 large yellow onions, coarsely chopped

3 tbsp tomato paste

6 cloves garlic, smashed

6 fresh thyme sprigs
or ½ tsp dried thyme

3 bay leaves

3 cups (750 ml) fruity red wine, such as Zinfandel

3–4 cups (750 ml–1 l) beef consommé or broth, heated

1 recipe Carrot-Apple Purée (page 167)

¼ cup (⅓ oz/10 g) finely chopped fresh flat-leaf parsley

Grated zest of 1 lemon

serves 6

Place the short ribs in a large bowl and season all over with 1 tsp salt, pepper to taste, and the fennel (if using). Cover and refrigerate for at least 4 hours or preferably overnight. Let the ribs stand at room temperature for 30 minutes.

Preheat the oven to 475°F (245°C).

Arrange the ribs, bone side down, in a deep roasting pan just large enough to hold them without crowding. Roast until lightly browned, about 20 minutes.

Meanwhile, in a large sauté pan, warm the olive oil over medium heat. Add the onions and cook, stirring occasionally, until lightly browned, about 8 minutes. Add the tomato paste, garlic, thyme, and bay leaves and cook, stirring occasionally, for 2 minutes.

Transfer the ribs to a platter and wipe out the fat in the roasting pan with a paper towel. Spread the onion mixture in the pan and arrange the ribs, bone sides up, on top. Pour in the wine and enough hot consommé to barely cover the meat, leaving the bones uncovered. Cover the pan tightly with aluminum foil and roast until the liquid begins to simmer, about 20 minutes. Reduce the oven temperature to 350°F (180°C) and braise for 2¼ hours, then test for doneness. The meat should be very tender and nearly falling off the bones. If not yet done, braise 15–45 minutes longer. Transfer to a platter, tent with the foil, and keep warm.

Pour the juices and vegetables from the pan into a large fine-mesh sieve set over a large measuring cup or fat separator. Press down firmly on the vegetable mixture to extract all the juices; discard the vegetables. Let the juices settle, then skim off the fat. Transfer the juices to a small saucepan, place over medium-high heat, and simmer until reduced by about two-thirds, 10–15 minutes. Season with salt and pepper; if you used consommé, there is no need to add salt.

Trim off and discard the rib bones, leaving the meat mostly intact. Divide the purée among warmed shallow bowls and place a short rib on top. Drizzle the edges of each bowl with a little of the reduced juices. Sprinkle with the parsley and a pinch of lemon zest and serve. Pass the remaining juices at the table.

Roasted Pork Shoulder with Sweet Potatoes & Pomegranate

The technique known as the "reverse sear," in which a roast is cooked in a low oven to the desired doneness temperature and then blasted in a superhot oven to a beautiful brown, is an excellent method for cooking pork shoulder.

About 6 hours before you plan to serve the pork, let it stand at room temperature for 1 hour. In a small bowl, stir together the cumin, garlic powder, 1½ tsp salt, and 1 tbsp of the olive oil. Place the pork on a large rimmed baking sheet and rub the seasoning mixture all over the meat, working it into the nooks and crannies.

Preheat the oven to 250°F (120°C). Insert an ovenproof thermometer into the thickest part of the meat from one side and prop the dial on a long edge of the pan. Place the roast in the oven with the dial facing the glass on the oven door. Slow-roast the pork without opening the door until the internal temperature registers 180°F (82°C), about 4 hours (don't be alarmed if the temperature stalls for up to 35 minutes around the 160°F/71°C mark). Remove the pork from the oven and turn the oven off. Let the pork rest at room temperature, uncovered, for 30–40 minutes. (Don't skip this step; it's a great time to attend to other cooking chores.)

Meanwhile, in a steamer basket set over a large saucepan of simmering water, steam the sweet potatoes until just tender, about 8 minutes. Turn out onto a kitchen towel and let stand for 5 minutes. Transfer the sweet potatoes to a large bowl. Sprinkle with the allspice, turmeric, and ½ tsp salt, drizzle with the remaining 1 tbsp olive oil, and stir gently until evenly coated.

Preheat the oven to 475°F (245°C). Place the pork, fatty side up, in the center of a clean baking sheet and surround it with the sweet potatoes in a single layer. Roast until the meat is crispy and caramelized and the sweet potatoes are crisped, 11–13 minutes.

There is no need to let the roast rest. Immediately transfer it to a carving board and cut across the grain into slices about ¼ inch (6 mm) thick. Top the pork with the sweet potatoes, scatter with the pomegranate seeds, drizzle with a little fig balsamic vinegar, and serve.

3½–4 lb (1.75–2 kg) boneless pork shoulder (Boston butt), trimmed of excess fat

1 tsp ground cumin

1 tsp garlic powder

Salt and freshly ground pepper

2 tbsp olive oil

2 lb (1 kg) sweet potatoes, peeled and cut into ¾-inch (2-cm) chunks

½ tsp ground allspice

½ tsp ground turmeric

1 cup (4 oz/125 g) pomegranate seeds

Fig balsamic vinegar for drizzling

serves 6

ADD FRESH FLAVOR
Brighten each serving with an
herb garnish. Try a last-minute
sprinkling of chopped fresh sage
or some delicate sprigs of thyme.

Pan-Seared Sea Bass with Acorn Squash

Braising vegetables in shallow liquid with a little sugar and butter is a classic French technique that I have adapted here for fall-friendly acorn squash. A Delicata, kabocha, Red Kuri, or Sweet Dumpling squash would be delicious, too.

Cut the squash in half lengthwise, then scoop out and discard the seeds. Cut each half crosswise. Cut each quarter into crescents 1½ inch (4 cm) thick, then cut each crescent in half.

In a sauté pan, combine the squash, vermouth, and Lillet Blanc and season with salt and pepper. Place over high heat and bring to a boil. Reduce the heat to low, cover, and simmer for 5 minutes. Uncover the pan, raise the heat to medium-low, and simmer until the liquid has completely evaporated but the squash has not yet begun to scorch, 8–10 minutes. Add the 1 tbsp butter and the walnuts and cook, shaking the pan and turning the squash over occasionally, until the squash is golden brown and tender, 5–7 minutes. Gently fold in the sage and remove from the heat.

Pat the fish fillets dry with paper towels. Season the tops of the fillets lightly with salt and pepper and dust with flour. In a large nonstick frying pan, melt the 2 tsp butter with the grapeseed oil over medium-high heat. When the foam subsides, add the fillets, floured side down, and sear without moving them for 2 minutes. Season lightly with salt and pepper and dust with flour, then carefully turn the fish over and sear for 2 minutes. Reduce the heat to very low and cook until the fish is just firm to the touch and opaque at the center, 2–4 minutes longer.

Place a fish fillet in the center of each warmed plate, spoon some of the squash on top, and serve with lemon wedges, if you like.

1¼ lb (625 g) acorn squash, scrubbed

1 cup (250 ml) vermouth or medium-dry white wine, such as Viognier

2 tbsp Lillet Blanc or medium-dry sherry

Salt and freshly ground pepper

1 tbsp plus 2 tsp unsalted butter

½ cup (2 oz/60 g) coarsely chopped walnuts

1½ tbsp finely chopped fresh sage

4 sea bass or other whitefish fillets, about 1½ lb (750 g) total

Superfine or all-purpose flour for dusting

1 tbsp grapeseed or canola oil

Lemon wedges for serving (optional)

serves 4

Autumnal Squashes

Most cool-weather squashes have thick skins and dense, sweet flesh and can be stored in a cool, dark place for several weeks. Look for specimens that are firm to the touch, feel heavy for their size, are free of gashes or soft patches, have matte skin, and a dry, solidly anchored stem. If you must remove the skin before cooking, use a sturdy, sharp vegetable peeler or paring knife.

GOLDEN ACORN

BUTTERNUT

BUTTERCUP

KABOCHA

DELICATA

SWEET DUMPLING

GOLDEN NUGGET

Cider-Braised Chicken Legs with Fresh Figs & Cipollini Onions

Soft, plump figs have a relatively short shelf life, so are best eaten soon after they ripen. With luck, you will be able to put this classic braise on the menu during fig season, which typically stretches from late summer through October.

4 whole chicken legs, about ¼ lb (125 g) each

Salt and freshly ground pepper

2 tbsp olive oil

2 large shallots, coarsely chopped

1 large fresh rosemary sprig, plus ¾ tsp minced fresh rosemary

1 large fresh thyme sprig

1¼ cups (310 ml) hard apple cider

¾ cup (180 ml) chicken broth

1 lemon slice

12 cipollini onions, about ½ lb (250 g) total, peeled

9 fresh figs, about 1 lb (500 g) total, stemmed and halved lengthwise

1 tbsp whole-grain mustard

2 tbsp cold unsalted butter, cut into 4 pieces

serves 4–6

Preheat the oven to 325°F (165°C).

Pat the chicken legs dry with paper towels. Season generously with salt and pepper. Let stand at room temperature for 20 minutes.

In a large ovenproof sauté pan or Dutch oven, warm the olive oil over medium-high heat. Working in batches, add the chicken and cook until golden brown on all sides, turning occasionally, 5–7 minutes. Transfer to a platter. Reduce the heat to medium-low and add the shallots and rosemary and thyme sprigs. Cook, stirring occasionally, until the shallots are tender, about 5 minutes. Add the cider, raise the heat to medium-high, and bring to a brisk simmer. Simmer until the liquid is reduced by about half, 6–8 minutes.

Return the chicken, skin side up, to the pan and add the broth, lemon slice, ¼ tsp salt, and plenty of pepper. Bring to a simmer, then cover the pan and transfer to the oven. Cook for 15 minutes, then add the onions and minced rosemary. Cover and continue to cook until the chicken is very tender and an instant-read thermometer inserted into the thickest part of a thigh, away from the bone, registers 160°F (71°C), about 10 minutes longer. Using tongs, transfer the chicken to a platter and keep warm in the turned-off oven with the door slightly ajar. Remove and discard the herb sprigs and lemon slice.

Place the pan over medium-high heat and simmer, stirring occasionally, until the liquid is reduced by about half, about 5 minutes. Add the figs and simmer for about 3 minutes; the fig halves should remain intact. Remove the pan from the heat and add the mustard and butter, swirling the pan until the butter has emulsified.

Serve the chicken legs whole or cut in half and top with the figs, onions, and sauce.

Apple Fritters with Cinnamon Cream

For easy frying, have ready a deep-frying thermometer and two sets of tongs—one for dipping the slices in the batter and the other for lifting them from the oil. If the apples are large, fry only four slices at a time so they cook and crisp properly.

To make the cinnamon cream, in a small bowl, whisk together the crème fraîche, granulated sugar, and cinnamon. Add more sugar and/or cinnamon to taste. Refrigerate until ready to serve.

In a bowl, whisk together the flour, granulated sugar, baking powder, cinnamon, nutmeg, and salt. In a liquid measuring cup, whisk together the egg and buttermilk. Make a well in the flour mixture and pour in the egg mixture, whisking around the sides of the well to slowly incorporate the wet ingredients with the dry; don't overmix. Set the batter aside.

Peel the apples if desired. Cut the apples crosswise into slices slightly more than ¼ inch (6 mm) thick. You should have about 6 slices per apple. Use a small cookie cutter to punch out the center core and form neat rings.

In a large, deep pot, pour in vegetable oil to a depth of 1½ inches (4 cm) and heat over medium heat to 350°F (180°C) on a deep-frying thermometer. Line 2 rimmed baking sheets with paper towels.

Dredge 2 apple slices in the batter, letting the excess drip off, and carefully lower into the hot oil. Quickly repeat with 2–4 more slices; do not overcrowd. Fry, turning the fritters occasionally, until evenly browned, 1–1½ minutes on each side. Using tongs, transfer to the prepared baking sheet. Repeat to fry the remaining apple slices.

Dust the fritters with confectioners' sugar and serve warm with the cinnamon cream for dipping.

FOR THE CINNAMON CREAM

¾ cup (6 oz/185 g) crème fraîche or whipped cream

½ tsp granulated sugar, plus more as needed

¼–½ tsp ground cinnamon

1 cup (5 oz/155 g) all-purpose flour

2 tbsp granulated sugar

¼ tsp baking powder

½ tsp ground cinnamon

¼ tsp ground nutmeg

¼ tsp salt

1 large egg

1¼ cups (310 ml) buttermilk

2 large apples, such as Fuji or Gala

Vegetable oil for frying

Confectioners' sugar for dusting

makes about 12 fritters

SERVE Á LA MODE

You can skip the dollop of crème fraîche in favor of a scoop of ice cream in your flavor of choice. Brown butter, salted caramel, ginger, cinnamon, or vanilla bean are good options.

Pear, Quince & Apple Galette

If using a Pink Lady or Cortland apple for this free-form tart, you won't need to peel it, as their skin is thin. A thicker-skinned pie apple, such as a Rome or Stayman Winesap, will need peeling.

Prepare the dough. Set aside.

In a saucepan, melt the butter over medium-low heat. Add the quinces, cover, and cook gently until very tender, 20–25 minutes. Scatter 1 tbsp of the brown sugar over the quinces, then transfer to a food processor and purée until smooth, or mash with a potato masher.

Preheat the oven to 350°F (180°C). Line a large rimless baking sheet with parchment paper and sprinkle with a little flour.

Working directly on the parchment, roll out the dough into a 14-inch (35-cm) round about ⅛ inch (3 mm) thick. Spread the quince purée over the dough, leaving a 2-inch (5-cm) uncovered border, and scatter with the currants. Layer the pear and apple slices in concentric circles on top, alternating the slices and making sure the apple skin is visible. Fold in the edges of the dough to partly cover the outer 1 inch (2.5 cm) or so of the fruit, pleating the dough as you fold. Brush the exposed dough with a little beaten egg and sprinkle the remaining 1 tbsp sugar over the fruit.

Bake until the pastry is golden and the fruit is tender, 40–45 minutes. Let cool for 5 minutes, then brush the fruit evenly with the jelly. Scatter the crumbled macaroons on top (if using). Serve warm or at room temperature, spooning a dollop of crème fraîche atop each slice.

1 recipe Almond Tart Dough (page 166), at cool room temperature

2 tbsp unsalted butter

3 small quinces, peeled, cored, and cut into ¾-inch (2-cm) chunks

2 tbsp firmly packed golden brown sugar

All-purpose flour for dusting

1 tbsp currants or dried cranberries

1 firm but ripe Bosc pear, cored, and cut into ¼-inch (6-mm) slices

1 large red cooking apple, preferably Pink Lady or Cortland, cored and cut into ¼-inch (6-mm) slices

1 large egg, lightly beaten

¼ cup (2 oz/60 g) apple jelly or seedless raspberry jam, warmed with 1 tbsp water

2–3 Amaretti di Saronno macaroons, crumbled (optional)

⅓ cup (3 oz/90 g) crème fraîche

makes one 12-inch (30-cm) galette; serves 8–10

Pumpkin Tart with Gingersnap Crust

Pumpkins are icons of the fall season. For this tart, a thin layer of spiced pumpkin purée is poured over a layer of crisp and buttery crushed gingersnaps, and the result is a tantalizing mix of creamy and crunchy, spicy and sweet.

FOR THE CRUST

4 tbsp (2 oz/60 g) unsalted butter, melted and cooled, plus more butter for greasing

40 (10 oz/315 g) hard store-bought gingersnap cookies

FOR THE PUMPKIN FILLING

1 can (14 oz/440 g) pumpkin purée, or 1¾ cups (440 g) homemade purée (page 167)

¾ cup (6 oz/185 g) sugar

½ tsp salt

1 tsp ground cinnamon

½ tsp ground ginger

½ tsp freshly grated nutmeg

¼ tsp ground cloves

2 large eggs

1 cup (250 ml) evaporated milk

serves 8–10

Preheat the oven to 325°F (160°C).

To make the crust, grease an 11-inch (28-cm) tart pan with a removable bottom with butter. In a food processor, process the cookies to fine crumbs. Add the melted butter and process until the crumbs are moistened. Pour the crumbs into the prepared tart pan and press evenly and firmly over the bottom and up the sides of the pan. Bake just until set, 8–10 minutes. Let cool on a wire rack.

To make the filling, in a large saucepan, cook the pumpkin purée over medium heat, stirring occasionally, until it begins to caramelize, about 5 minutes. Remove from the heat and stir in the sugar, salt, cinnamon, ginger, nutmeg, and cloves. In a bowl, whisk together the eggs and evaporated milk. Whisk the egg mixture into the pumpkin mixture.

Place the tart shell on a baking sheet and pour the filling into the tart shell. Bake the tart for 15 minutes. Reduce the oven temperature to 300°F (150°C) and continue to bake until just the center jiggles slightly when the pan is gently shaken, about 30 minutes longer. Transfer to a wire rack and let cool for at least 20 minutes before serving.

Roasted Figs with Mascarpone

When figs are at their peak, they need very little embellishment for the ultimate in rich flavor. Roasting them with a sprinkling of brown sugar brings out their full sweetness. Mascarpone flecked with orange zest is a lovely partner to the figs.

Preheat the broiler. Line a baking sheet with aluminum foil.

In a bowl, whisk together the cheese, orange zest, and triple sec (if using). Set aside.

Place the figs, cut side up, on the prepared baking sheet and sprinkle each half evenly with ¼ tsp of the brown sugar. Broil until the sugar is molten brown and bubbling, 2–3 minutes, watching carefully and rotating the pan if needed to help the figs brown evenly.

Spread about 2 tbsp of the cheese mixture in the center of each of 6 plates. Place 2 fig halves, cut side up, on top. Sprinkle with the orange zest and the remaining 1 tsp brown sugar and serve.

6 oz (185 g) very cold mascarpone cheese

Grated zest of 1 orange

1 tsp triple sec or Cointreau (optional)

6 firm but ripe fresh figs, halved through the stems

4 tsp firmly packed dark brown sugar

serves 6

A Salad for Every Season

Radish + Pea

4 oz (125 g) radishes, thinly sliced

4 oz (125 g) snow peas and sugar snap peas

2 heads Belgian endive, thinly sliced crosswise

½ cup (½ oz/15 g) watercress sprigs

Vinaigrette of choice

Salt and freshly ground pepper

In a bowl, combine the radishes, snow peas, sugar snap peas, and endive. Toss to mix. Sprinkle the watercress over the top and drizzle with the vinaigrette. Toss to coat evenly, season to taste with salt and pepper, and serve.

Green Bean + Cherry Tomato

1 head Boston or butter lettuce, separated into leaves

2 cups (12 oz/375 g) cherry tomatoes, halved

1 avocado, pitted, peeled, and sliced

8 oz (250 g) green beans, blanched and cooled

¼ cup (¼ oz/7 g) fresh cilantro leaves

Vinaigrette of choice

Salt and freshly ground pepper

Line the bottoms of four individual salad bowls with lettuce leaves. Divide the cherry tomatoes, avocado, and green beans evenly among the bowls. Sprinkle evenly with the cilantro leaves. Drizzle with the vinaigrette, season to taste with salt and pepper, and serve.

Salads are ideal for adding seasonal texture and color to your table. Here are four recipes to get you started, each of them loaded with both flavor and nutrients. Each recipe serves four. Feel free to swap in what looks good at the market, such as a different green for the chard or sugar snaps for the snow peas.

Chard + Squash

1 small winter squash, such as Sweet Dumpling, acorn, or golden

2 small beets, trimmed

1 tbsp olive oil

1 bunch Swiss chard, tough ribs removed and leaves torn

Red wine vinaigrette or vinaigrette of choice

Salt and freshly ground pepper

Cut the winter squash into wedges and remove the seeds, if desired. Transfer the wedges to a baking dish. Halve the beets and add to the dish. Drizzle with the oil and toss to coat. Bake in a preheated 450°F (230°C) oven, stirring once, until tender and lightly browned, 20–40 minutes. Let cool. Peel and slice the beets. Place the chard in a bowl, drizzle with some of the vinaigrette. Toss to coat. Add the squash and beets, drizzle with the remaining vinaigrette, and season to taste with salt and pepper.

Mushroom + Brussels Sprout

12 oz (375 g) brussels sprouts, trimmed and halved

8 oz (250 g) mixed mushrooms, trimmed and sliced

1 tbsp olive oil

2 tsp chopped fresh thyme

Salt and freshly ground pepper

1½ cups (9 oz/285 g) cooked wheat berries

Balsamic vinaigrette or vinaigrette of choice

Place the brussels sprouts and mushrooms in separate piles on a rimmed baking sheet. Drizzle each pile evenly with the olive oil and toss to coat. Sprinkle with thyme, season with salt and pepper, and spread out into an even layer. Bake in a preheated 450°F (230°C) oven, stirring once, until tender and lightly browned, about 20 minutes. In a bowl, combine the wheat berries, brussels sprouts, and mushrooms. Drizzle with the vinaigrette, adjust the seasonings, and toss to mix.

WINTER

Roots, tubers, and chicories join the burgeoning show of brassicas in winter markets, sharing space with persimmons, pears, citrus, and pomegranates. With the onset of colder weather, cooks turn on the oven for everything from roasted parsnips to pizza to crème brûlée.

EXPLORE WINTER ROOTS
Instead of beets, roast baby carrots in a colorful mix—red, orange, white, and/or purple—or double up on your roots, combining beets and carrots.

Roasted Red & Yellow Beets with Burrata, Sherry Vinaigrette & Escarole

Roasting beets heightens their natural sugars, giving them a richer caramelized flavor and a smooth, silky texture. Look for beets in a mix of colors, including red-and-white-striped baby Chioggia beets, for the prettiest plate.

Preheat the oven to 350°F (180°C). Wrap each beet securely in a square of aluminum foil and bake until tender when pierced with a knife, 35–45 minutes. Cool, peel, and slice into wedges.

To make the vinaigrette, in a large bowl, whisk the vinegar, shallot, mustard, honey, salt, and pepper until smooth. Drizzle in the oil, whisking until emulsified. Reserve about one-fourth of the dressing.

Add the escarole to the bowl and toss until well combined. On a platter or individual plates, make a layer of the dressed escarole, reserving a few leaves for garnish. Layer the sliced beets over the escarole and scatter with the burrata. Drizzle the beets and burrata with the reserved dressing and scatter with the reserved escarole. Season with pepper and serve at once.

7 baby red and/or yellow beets, trimmed and scrubbed

FOR THE VINAIGRETTE

2 tbsp sherry vinegar

1 small shallot, finely chopped

1 tsp Dijon mustard

1½ tsp honey

¼ tsp fine sea salt

⅛ tsp freshly ground pepper

⅓ cup (80 ml) extra-virgin olive oil

4 cups (4 oz/125 g) winter greens, such as escarole, arugula, frisée, and radicchio

½ lb (250 g) very fresh burrata, pulled into small chunks

Freshly ground pepper

serves 6

Roasted Oysters with Sriracha-Lime Butter

Purists insist that oysters must be eaten raw or not at all, but the brilliant alchemy used here of very little heat is certain to win converts. Oysters are best in the cold-weather months, when they are plumper and taste more fully of the sea.

FOR THE BUTTER

4 tbsp (2 oz/60 g) salted butter, at room temperature

1–1½ tsp Sriracha or other hot sauce, or to taste

½ small shallot, minced

Grated zest of 1 small lime

1 tbsp fresh lime juice

2 tsp finely snipped fresh chives

24 oysters
Rock salt for serving

serves 4–6

To prepare the butter, in a small bowl, mash together the butter, Sriracha, shallot, lime zest and juice, and chives. Cover and refrigerate for at least 1 hour or up to 24 hours. If refrigerated for more than 4 hours, let stand at room temperature for about 10 minutes before serving.

Preheat the oven to 475°F (245°C). Place a flat wire rack on a large rimmed baking sheet. Pour a layer of rock salt on a serving platter.

Discard any oysters that do not close tightly to the touch. To shuck the oysters, scrub each one thoroughly with a stiff-bristled brush, rinsing it well under cold running water. Holding each oyster flat-side up in a kitchen towel and using an oyster knife, slip the tip of the knife into the shell near the hinge and pry upward to open. Run the knife blade along the inside of the top shell to sever the muscle that joins the shells, then lift off the top shell. Run the knife underneath the oyster to free it from the rounded, bottom shell, being careful not to spill the liquor.

Arrange the oysters, open side up, on the rack and pour a generous ¼ inch (6 mm) of hot water into the baking sheet. Roast until the oyster liquor begins to sizzle, 7–9 minutes. Using gloves or tongs, transfer the oysters to the rock salt–lined platter without spilling the liquor. Immediately top each oyster with ½ tsp of the Sriracha-lime butter and serve.

Crostini with Radicchio, Smoked Trout & Horseradish Cream

Purple-red radicchio is prized for its color and earthy bitterness, two qualities that dissipate as soon as it is cooked. Here, I sear the radicchio only briefly, just long enough to add a little smoky flavor and to wilt the leaves slightly.

Preheat the oven to 350°F (180°C).

Arrange the baguette slices on a baking sheet. Coat the tops lightly with olive oil, and season lightly with salt and black pepper. Bake until golden, 10–15 minutes. Transfer to a serving platter and rub each crostini lightly with the cut side of the garlic clove. Set aside.

In a small bowl, whisk together the crème fraîche, horseradish, mayonnaise, and ⅛ tsp white pepper. Set aside.

Preheat a large cast-iron frying pan or griddle pan over high heat and coat it lightly with olive oil cooking spray. Dip the radicchio briefly in water and shake off the excess. Season the cut side lightly with salt. When the pan is very hot, place the radicchio, cut side down, in the pan and cook until slightly charred, 1½–2 minutes. Turn and sear on the rounded side for 15 seconds. Transfer to a cutting board and let cool, then cut crosswise into slivers.

Place a pinch of radicchio on each crostini and top with about 2 tsp of the horseradish cream, spreading it out slightly to make an even bed for the trout. Top each crostini with several flakes of smoked trout, sprinkle with the tarragon, and serve.

12–14 slices sourdough baguette, each ½ inch (12 mm) thick

2 tbsp olive oil, or nonstick olive oil cooking spray

Salt and freshly ground black pepper

1 clove garlic, halved lengthwise

½ cup (4 oz/125 g) crème fraîche or sour cream

1 tbsp prepared horseradish

1 tbsp mayonnaise

Freshly ground white pepper

½ head radicchio, halved lengthwise through the core

7 oz (220 g) smoked trout, flaked

1 tbsp minced fresh tarragon and/or finely snipped fresh chives

makes 12–14 crostini;
serves 4–6

Creamy Cauliflower Soup with Brussels Sprout Hash

Two common cool-weather brassicas come together in this simple soup that is special enough for a dinner party. Although white cauliflower is the most common type available, other colors can be substituted.

2 tbsp olive oil

1 yellow onion, diced

4 shallots, sliced

3 ribs celery, diced

1 head cauliflower, about 2½ lb (1.25 kg), trimmed and cut into florets

Salt and freshly ground pepper

5 cups (1.25 l) chicken or vegetable broth, plus more as needed

FOR THE HASH

¼ lb (125 g) pancetta, diced

1 large shallot, halved and thinly sliced

⅓ lb (155 g) brussels sprouts, sliced ¼ inch (6 mm) thick

1 tbsp olive oil

Salt and freshly ground pepper

1 tbsp fresh lemon juice

¾ cup (180 ml) heavy cream (optional)

serves 6

Preheat the oven to 350°F (180°C).

In a large pot, warm the olive oil over medium heat. Add the onion, shallots, and celery and cook, stirring occasionally, until softened, 8–10 minutes. Add the cauliflower and cook, stirring occasionally, for 1–2 minutes. Season with salt and pepper. Add the broth, raise the heat to medium-high, and bring to a boil. Reduce the heat to medium-low, cover, and simmer until the cauliflower is tender, about 30 minutes. Remove from the heat and let cool slightly.

Meanwhile, make the hash: In a frying pan, cook the pancetta over medium heat, stirring frequently, until most of the fat is rendered, about 4 minutes (it will not be fully cooked). Add the shallot, raise the heat to medium-high, and cook, stirring occasionally, until the shallot is soft and beginning to turn golden, about 4 minutes. Add the brussels sprouts and olive oil, season with salt and pepper, and cook, stirring frequently, until the sprouts are fork-tender, about 6 minutes. Set aside.

In a blender or food processor, working in batches if necessary, process the soup until smooth. Return the soup to the pot and reheat over medium heat, adding more broth if needed to reach the desired consistency. Season to taste with salt and pepper. Stir in the lemon juice and cream (if using). Ladle the soup into warmed bowls, garnish with the brussels sprout hash, and serve.

ADD A SPLASH OF COLOR
If you decide to go for color, choose a vibrant orange or purple cauliflower—both stay bright when cooked—to contrast with the brussels sprout garnish.

Oven-Roasted Ricotta with Citrus & Pomegranate

The success of this delightfully simple recipe depends on using thick, rich fresh whole-milk ricotta, preferably locally made. If a supermarket brand is your only option, drain it overnight in a sieve lined with a double layer of cheesecloth.

2 cups (1 lb/500 g) whole-milk ricotta cheese, at room temperature

1½ tbsp pure maple syrup

1 tsp minced fresh sage

1 tsp grated orange or lemon zest

½ tsp ground fennel

¼ tsp salt

¼ tsp freshly ground pepper

½ cup (2 oz/60 g) pomegranate seeds

Citrus-infused extra-virgin olive oil, preferably orange, for drizzling

Crostini or fruit and nut crisps for serving

serves 4

Preheat the oven to 475°F (245°C).

In a bowl, whisk together the cheese, maple syrup, sage, orange zest, fennel, salt, and pepper. Scoop the cheese into a small, shallow gratin dish and rough up the surface to create nice peaks for browning. Roast until firm and charred on the peaks and edges, about 25 minutes.

Scatter the pomegranate seeds on top and drizzle with citrus olive oil. Serve warm as a spread, with crostini on the side.

Potato & Pancetta Crostata with Fresh Rosemary

This savory crostata might look like a pizza, but the similarity ends there. The crust is buttery pastry, and the filling is more like that of a quiche. Serve it with a salad of winter greens—escarole, arugula, radicchio, endive—and a crisp white wine.

To make the pastry, in a food processor, combine the flour, salt, and butter and pulse until small crumbs form. In a measuring cup, whisk together the egg and ice water. With the motor running, quickly pour in the egg mixture and pulse just until the mixture comes together into a rough mass. If it takes more than about 20 seconds to clump together, add a little more ice water and pulse again.

Transfer the pastry to a lightly floured surface and shape into a smooth disk. Wrap with plastic wrap and refrigerate for 30 minutes or up to 1 day.

Preheat the oven to 400°F (200°C).

In a large frying pan, melt the butter with the grapeseed oil over medium heat. When the foam subsides, add the onion and ½ tsp salt. Cook, stirring occasionally, until the onion is tender and golden brown (even a bit charred in places), 10–12 minutes. Let cool completely.

In a large bowl, stir together the cream, nutmeg, garlic, ¾ tsp salt, and plenty of pepper. Working quickly, use a mandoline to shave the potatoes about ⅛ inch (3 mm) thick and add to the bowl. Using your hands, mix the potato slices thoroughly with the cream, coating them evenly.

On a large piece of parchment paper, roll out the pastry into a 10-inch (25-cm) round; don't worry if the edges are uneven. Slide the parchment onto a large baking sheet. Spread the caramelized onion over the pastry in a thin, even layer, leaving a ½-inch (12-mm) uncovered border. Slightly overlap the potato slices in concentric circles over the onion, keeping them ½ inch (12 mm) within the onion border. Drizzle the remaining cream mixture from the bowl over the potatoes. Arrange the pancetta strips on top.

Bake until the edges of the pastry are lightly golden, the pancetta is crispy, and the potatoes are tender, 30–35 minutes. Sprinkle the crostata with the rosemary, then cut into slices and serve.

FOR THE PASTRY

2¼ cups (9 oz/280 g) all-purpose flour, plus more for dusting

½ tsp salt

½ cup (4 oz/125 g) cold unsalted butter, cut into small cubes

1 large egg

3 tbsp ice water, plus more as needed

1 tbsp butter

1 tbsp grapeseed or canola oil

1 large white or yellow onion, coarsely chopped

Salt and freshly ground pepper

⅓ cup (80 ml) plus 1 tbsp heavy cream

Pinch of ground nutmeg

4 cloves garlic, minced

4 small red potatoes, about 6 oz (185 g) total

3 oz (90 g) thinly sliced pancetta, cut into 1-inch (2.5-cm) strips

2 tsp minced fresh rosemary

makes one 10-inch (25-cm) tart; serves about 4

VERSATILE ROOTS
Use other seasonal root
vegetables for making oven
fries, such as daikon, turnips,
rutabagas, sweet potatoes,
or even year-round yucca.

Parsnip Oven Fries with Chile-Spiced Crème Fraîche

In England, where I lived for a time, slender, creamy white parsnips were regularly included on Sunday lunch and weeknight supper menus during the winter months. They make great oven fries, especially when tossed with duck fat for roasting.

Preheat the oven to 425°F (220°C).

Cut the parsnips in half lengthwise. (Alternatively, cut the parsnips in half lengthwise and then crosswise into pieces about 1 inch (2.5 cm) long. The pieces from the tapered end will be much smaller than the ones from the top. That's okay.)

Bring a large saucepan of lightly salted water to a boil over high heat. Add the parsnips and cook until almost tender 3-4 minutes. Drain well and rinse with running cold water, then drain thoroughly .

Arrange the parsnips in a single layer in a large baking dish. Drizzle with the duck fat and toss to coat evenly. Season with salt and pepper and drizzle with the honey. Roast until the parsnips are tender, 40-45 minutes. Turn the oven to its highest heat (usually 550°F/290°C) and roast until the parsnips are shiny and crisp, 5-10 minutes longer.

In a small bowl, whisk together the crème fraîche, chile powder, and lime juice. Drizzle the parsnips with a little crème fraîche and sprinkle with the lime zest. Serve the remaining crème fraîche on the side.

1½–2 lb (750 g–1 kg) parsnips

Salt and freshly ground pepper

3 tbsp duck fat, bacon drippings, or olive oil

3 tbsp honey

½ cup (4 oz/125 g) crème fraîche

½–1 tsp mild or hot chile powder, preferably chipotle chile powder

Finely grated zest of 1 lime plus 1 tbsp fresh lime juice

serves 4–6

Winter Vegetables

In the cold months, dense, sturdy roots and tubers reign on dinner menus. Many of them, including potatoes, sweet potatoes, rutabagas, and turnips, will keep in a dark, cool, well-ventilated place for weeks, while others, such as carrots, beets, celery roots, and parsnips, must be refrigerated. They share the winter table with hard-skinned squashes, another good keeper, and nutrient-rich brussels sprouts, cabbages, and other brassicas.

RUTABAGA

WATERMELON
RADISH

BRUSSELS SPROUTS

CHIOGGIA BEET

CHERRY
BELLE
RADISHES

TURNIPS

RED CABBAGE

FRENCH
BREAKFAST
RADISHES

PURPLE CARROTS

Mushroom Soup with Crispy Prosciutto & Marjoram

To have the components of this creamy, rustic soup ready at the same time, slip the prosciutto into the oven, then immediately begin making the soup. If the prosciutto seems too oily when it emerges, drain it briefly on paper towels before crumbling it.

4 thin slices prosciutto

4 tbsp (2 oz/60 g) butter

4 tbsp (60 ml) olive oil

1½ lb (750 g) assorted wild or cultivated mushrooms, such as cremini, shiitake, maitake, and/or baby bellas, trimmed, brushed clean, and thickly sliced

Salt and freshly ground pepper

2 tsp minced fresh marjoram

4 shallots, chopped

1 large leek, white and pale green parts, thinly sliced

4 cloves garlic, minced or pushed through a press

½ cup (125 ml) Madeira wine or medium-dry sherry

4 cups (1 l) low-sodium chicken broth

1¼ cups (310 ml) heavy cream

1 bay leaf

3 fresh thyme sprigs

serves 6

Preheat the oven to 300°F (150°C). Line a baking sheet with parchment paper. Place the prosciutto on the prepared baking sheet. Cover with another sheet of parchment, then with a baking sheet that sits flat on top of the paper. Bake until the prosciutto is golden brown and crisp, 45–50 minutes. Set aside.

Meanwhile, in a large pot, melt 1 tbsp of the butter with 1 tbsp of the olive oil over medium-high heat. Add one-third of the mushrooms and cook without stirring until browned underneath, 3–4 minutes. Stir the mushrooms and continue to cook, stirring occasionally, until browned on both sides and tender, 3–4 minutes longer. Season with salt and pepper, transfer to a bowl, fold in the marjoram, and set aside for the garnish.

In the same pot, melt the remaining 3 tbsp butter with the remaining 3 tbsp olive oil over medium-low heat. Add the shallots and leek and cook, stirring occasionally, until the vegetables are softened but not browned, 4–6 minutes. Add the garlic and stir for 1 minute, then add the remaining mushrooms, raise the heat to medium-high, and cook, stirring frequently, until the mushrooms are shriveled and browned, 4–5 minutes more. Add the Madeira and cook, stirring occasionally, until most of the liquid has evaporated, 2–3 minutes. Add the broth, cream, ½ tsp salt, and ¼ tsp pepper. Add the bay leaf and thyme and bring to a boil. Adjust the heat so the soup simmers gently and cook, uncovered, until slightly thickened and the mushrooms are very tender, 20–25 minutes. Remove the thyme sprigs and bay leaf and let stand at room temperature for 5–10 minutes. Ladle most of the mushrooms and enough soup liquid into a blender to fill no more than three-fourths full. Place the lid on firmly and hold with a folded towel while you begin blending at the lowest speed. Blend until chunky-smooth, then return the soup to the pot and warm through.

Divide the soup among bowls and top with a spoonful of reserved herbed mushrooms. Crumble some crispy prosciutto shards over the top and serve at once.

Crab Cioppino

There are countless versions of this San Francisco seafood classic. Dungeness crab, in season in late November, is traditionally in the mix. Serve this hearty stew with a salad of winter greens, a sourdough loaf, and a good Zinfandel or Pinot Noir.

In a large pot, warm the olive oil over medium heat. Add the onions and bell peppers and cook, stirring occasionally, until just tender, 4–5 minutes. Add the garlic and cook, stirring occasionally, for 30 seconds. Add the bay leaves, tomatoes and their juices, and red and white wines and bring to a simmer. Partially cover the pot, reduce the heat to medium-low, and cook until thickened slightly, about 15 minutes.

Remove and discard the bay leaves. Add the oregano, thyme, whitefish, and clams, discarding any that do not close to the touch. Cover and cook over medium-low heat for 5 minutes. Add the crab and shrimp, cover, and cook until the shrimp and fish are opaque throughout and the clams have opened, 3–4 minutes. Discard any unopened clams. Stir in the Tabasco, season to taste with salt and pepper, and serve.

¼ cup (60 ml) olive oil

2 yellow onions, chopped

2 red bell peppers, seeded and chopped

4 cloves garlic, minced

2 bay leaves, broken in half

1 can (28 oz/875 g) diced tomatoes with juices

¾ cup (180 ml) dry red wine

½ cup (125 ml) dry white wine

2 tbsp chopped fresh oregano

2 tbsp chopped fresh thyme

¾ lb (375 g) firm whitefish fillets, such as halibut or monkfish, cut into 1-inch (2.5-cm) chunks

1 lb (500 g) littleneck or other small clams, scrubbed and soaked

1 lb (500 g) Dungeness crab claws, or ½ lb (250 g) Dungeness or other lump crabmeat, picked over for shell fragments

20 large shrimp, heads and legs removed, or peeled and deveined if desired

¼–½ tsp Tabasco or other hot pepper sauce

Salt and freshly ground pepper

serves 6

Mixed Citrus Salad with Mâche, Fennel & Celery

Winter is the height of citrus season, with an appealing display of oranges, mandarins, tangerines, tangelos, pomelos, and more in the best-stocked markets. Use a varied mixture of sweet-tart types for the prettiest, tastiest salad.

2 ribs celery

2 bunches mâche

2 lb (1 kg) mixed citrus fruits, such as navel oranges, blood oranges, tangerines, mandarins, and pomelos

½ fennel bulb, trimmed

8 kumquats

¼ cup (1 oz/30 g) sliced almonds, toasted

FOR THE VINAIGRETTE

Fresh orange juice, or as needed

1 tbsp Champagne vinegar

¼ cup (60 ml) extra-virgin olive oil

Salt and freshly ground pepper

serves 4

Cut the celery in half lengthwise. Using a serrated vegetable peeler or a mandoline, shave the celery into thin strips lengthwise down the ribs. Cut the strips in half crosswise and place in a bowl of water. Set aside.

Separate the mâche leaves and transfer to a shallow serving bowl. Working on a plate to capture all the juices, use a serrated knife to cut a thick slice off the top and bottom of each citrus fruit. Working with 1 fruit at a time, stand it upright and, following the contour of the fruit, carefully slice downward to remove the peel, pith, and membrane. Set the fruit on its side and cut crosswise into slices about ⅜ inch (1 cm) thick, discarding any seeds. Transfer the slices to the bowl with the mâche, reserving the juices for the vinaigrette.

Cut the fennel lengthwise in half. Using a mandoline or a sharp knife, cut the fennel crosswise into very thin slices and tuck among the citrus slices. Drain the celery and distribute evenly over the salad. Using the serrated knife, cut each kumquat crosswise into very thin slices, discarding any seeds. Scatter the kumquat slices evenly over the salad, then sprinkle the almonds over the top.

To make the vinaigrette, pour the reserved citrus juices into a measuring cup. Add enough additional orange juice to measure ½ cup (125 ml), then add the vinegar. Whisking constantly, slowly add the olive oil and whisk until well combined. Season to taste with salt and pepper. Drizzle the vinaigrette over the salad, toss gently to coat, and serve.

WINTER GREENS AT THEIR BEST
Mâche, also known as lamb's lettuce or corn salad, is a tender salad green prized for its nutty flavor and velvety texture. If unavailable, try young arugula or mixed baby greens instead.

Fuyu Persimmon Salad with Endive & Pomegranate

Bright orange Fuyu persimmons are crisp and colorful in winter salads. Don't confuse them with their cousin, the larger, more astringent, acorn-shaped Hachiya persimmon, which is nearly jelly-like when ready to eat.

FOR THE VINAIGRETTE

2 tbsp sherry vinegar

2 tsp minced shallot

1 tsp whole-grain mustard

Salt and freshly ground pepper

¼ cup (60 ml) extra-virgin olive oil

¼ cup (60 ml) walnut oil

2 cups (4 oz/125 g) baby arugula

2 heads Belgian endive, cut crosswise into ¼-inch (6-mm) slices

3 Fuyu persimmons

½ cup (2 oz/60 g) pomegranate seeds

½ cup (2 oz/60 g) walnuts, lightly toasted and coarsely chopped

serves 6

To make the vinaigrette, in a small bowl, whisk together the vinegar, shallot, mustard, and a pinch each of salt and pepper. Whisking constantly, slowly add the olive oil and walnut oil and whisk until well combined.

In a large bowl, combine the arugula and endive. Peel the persimmons and, using a mandoline or a sharp knife, shave into very thin slices, and transfer to the bowl. Add the pomegranate seeds, walnuts, and half of the vinaigrette and toss well. Add more vinaigrette as needed to lightly coat the greens and serve.

Warm Kale Salad with Lentils & Prosciutto

This warm salad is the ideal way to marry protein-rich lentils and nutrient-dense kale in a single dish. Beluga (black) lentils, which take on a beautiful shine and a deep ebony color when cooked, can be substituted for the French lentils.

In a large saucepan, warm the olive oil over medium heat. Add the carrots, onion, ¼ tsp salt, and several grindings of pepper and cook, stirring occasionally, until the onion is very soft and lightly caramelized, about 15 minutes. Add the kale and cook, stirring occasionally, until tender, about 6 minutes. Scrape the contents of the pan into a bowl and set aside. Wipe out the pan.

In the same saucepan, combine the lentils, thyme, garlic, broth, ½ tsp salt, and ¼ tsp pepper. Place over high heat and bring to a boil. Reduce the heat to medium and simmer until the lentils are tender but firm to the bite, 15–20 minutes.

Meanwhile, in a frying pan, cook the prosciutto over medium heat until crisp and browned, about 7 minutes. Let cool, then tear into small pieces.

Drain the lentils, remove and discard the thyme sprigs and garlic cloves, and return the lentils to the saucepan. Stir in the kale mixture and vinegar and season to taste with salt and pepper. Transfer the lentil mixture to a serving bowl, top with the prosciutto, and serve.

1 tbsp olive oil

4 carrots, about ¾ lb (350 g) total, peeled and diced

1 large red onion, thinly sliced

Salt and freshly ground pepper

1 large bunch Tuscan kale, tough stems removed and leaves thinly sliced

1 cup (7 oz/220 g) French green lentils, picked over and rinsed

2 fresh thyme sprigs

4 large cloves garlic

4 cups (1 l) chicken broth

6 thin slices prosciutto

1 tsp sherry vinegar

serves 6

BAKERS' TRICK
Parchment paper is the
novice pizza maker's
friend: shape the dough on
the paper, then slide the
dough and paper onto
the pizza steel or stone.

Pizza with Roasted Broccolini, Pancetta & Pine Nuts

As with most brassicas, broccolini's wonderfully mellow and nutty flavor is augmented by a light charring in a hot oven. Salty pancetta and rich pine nuts add to the depth of flavor, while tiny shards of lemon cut the richness.

Prepare the dough. Set aside.

Preheat the broiler.

In a bowl, toss together the broccolini, mayonnaise, and olive oil until evenly coated. Spread in a single layer on the prepared baking sheet. Broil, stirring once, until nicely charred but not blackened, 3–5 minutes. Set aside.

Place a heavy baking steel or pizza stone on the lower rack of the oven and preheat the oven to its highest setting (usually 550°F/290°C) for 30 minutes.

Trim the ends from the lemon and quarter lengthwise. Trim the lemon flesh, leaving about ⅛ inch (3 mm) attached to the peel (save the trimmed flesh for another use). Cut the quarters lengthwise into very thin wedges, then cut crosswise into tiny dice. You will need about 1½ tsp; save the rest for another use.

Line a large rimless baking sheet with parchment paper and dust with flour, or sprinkle cornmeal over a wooden pizza peel. Dust your hands with flour, then stretch and pull the dough into a 13-inch (33-cm) round (it doesn't have to be perfectly round) and place on the prepared baking sheet or pizza peel. Working quickly, brush the dough with a light coating of olive oil. Scatter the broccolini evenly over the dough and season generously with salt and pepper. Scatter the pancetta, diced lemon, pine nuts, and the cheese on top, leaving a 1-inch (2.5-cm) uncovered border.

Grasp the edges of the parchment paper with your fingers and carefully slide it from the baking sheet onto the very hot baking steel in the oven, or transfer the pizza to the baking steel with the pizza peel. Bake until the edges of the pizza are golden and the cheese is melty, 5–10 minutes. Pull the (now somewhat crumbly) parchment paper with the pizza onto the rimless baking sheet, or use the pizza peel to remove the pizza from the oven.

Transfer the pizza to a cutting board, cut into slices, and serve.

1 recipe Thin-Crust Dough (page 166), at room temperature

1 small bunch broccolini, trimmed and coarsely chopped

1 tbsp mayonnaise

1 tbsp olive oil, plus more for coating the dough

1 Meyer lemon

All-purpose flour or coarsely-ground cornmeal for dusting

Salt and freshly ground pepper

1½ oz (45 g) pancetta, diced

1 tbsp coarsely chopped pine nuts

3 oz (90 g) fresh mozzarella cheese, cut into small dice

makes one 13-inch (33-cm) pizza

Pasta with Brussels Sprout Leaves, Hazelnuts & Brown Butter

Two of my great winter solaces are, in order, roaring fires and brussels sprouts. Pulling apart the sprouts into individual leaves is time-consuming, so recruit a friend to help and pour some wine to make the job go more quickly.

6 tbsp (3 oz/90 g) unsalted butter

½ cup (2½ oz/75 g) hazelnuts, coarsely chopped

14 oz (440 g) brussels sprouts

1½ tbsp mayonnaise

2 tbsp olive oil

Salt and freshly ground pepper

2 thick slices pancetta, about 2½ oz (75 g) total, finely chopped

1 red onion, very thinly sliced

½ lb (250 g) penne pasta

serves 4

Preheat the broiler.

In a small saucepan, combine the butter and hazelnuts. Place over medium-high heat and melt the butter, swirling until foamy and nut brown. Remove from the heat and set aside.

Quarter the brussels sprouts through the core. Trim away the triangular core from each quarter, then break or pull apart into leaves. On a large rimmed baking sheet, toss together the brussels sprout leaves, mayonnaise, and 1 tbsp of the olive oil until evenly coated. Spread in an even layer and season generously with salt and pepper. Broil, tossing once, until nicely charred in places but not blackened, 3–5 minutes. Set aside.

In a large frying pan, warm the remaining 1 tbsp olive oil over medium-low heat. Add the pancetta, onion, and ½ tsp salt and cook, stirring occasionally, until the onion is softened, about 15 minutes. Remove from the heat.

Meanwhile, bring a large pot of generously salted water to a boil over high heat. Add the pasta and cook until al dente, about 9 minutes, or according to the package directions. Drain well, reserving ¼ cup (60 ml) of the cooking water. Add the cooking water to the pan with the onion and place over medium-low heat. Fold in the pasta and half of the brussels sprout leaves until blended and season generously with pepper. Heat until warmed through, about 1 minute, then transfer to a warmed platter or warmed individual plates.

Place the hazelnut butter over medium heat and quickly return to a sizzle. Spoon the bubbling butter and hazelnuts over the pasta. Scatter the remaining sprout leaves on top and serve.

Chile-Spiced Halibut with Frisée & Tangerine Salad

Poaching fish gently in oil yields beautifully tender, evenly cooked fillets. You do not need to use your best-quality olive oil here, and once the fish is cooked, let the oil cool and then refrigerate it for use in other fish recipes.

Finely grate the zest from 1 of the tangerines and set aside for garnish. Using a serrated knife, cut a thick slice off the top and bottom of each tangerine. Working with 1 fruit at a time, stand it upright and, following the contour of the fruit, carefully slice downward to remove the peel, pith, and membrane. Holding the fruit over a bowl to catch the juices, cut on either side of each segment to free it from the membrane. Squeeze the membrane to release the juice into the bowl. Cut the segments crosswise into small pieces, discarding any seeds. Set aside.

Add the vinegar, shallot, ¾ tsp salt, ½ tsp pepper, and the olive oil to the bowl with the tangerine juice and whisk until well combined. Stir in the tangerine segments and half of the chives. Set aside.

To prepare the halibut, in a small Dutch oven or heatproof casserole just large enough to hold the fish in a single layer, combine enough olive oil and grapeseed oil to just cover the fish, then add the rosemary, garlic, chipotle chiles, and ½ tsp salt. Place over medium heat and bring to a simmer. Remove from the heat and immediately slide the fish fillets into the oil, taking care that the oil doesn't splatter. Cover the pan and let stand for 7–9 minutes for medium-rare, or about 11 minutes for medium. An instant-read thermometer inserted into the center of each fillet should register 120°F (49°C) for medium-rare or 135°F (57°C) for medium.

Add the frisée to the bowl with the tangerines and toss to combine. Using a slotted spoon, transfer the fish, garlic, and chiles to warmed plates, discarding the rosemary sprigs. Sprinkle each fish fillet with a pinch of flaky sea salt and top with the salad. Season generously with pepper, sprinkle with the tangerine zest and the remaining chives, and serve.

2 large tangerines

1 tbsp rice vinegar

1 shallot, finely chopped

Salt and freshly ground pepper

3 tbsp extra-virgin olive oil

1½ tbsp finely snipped fresh chives

FOR THE HALIBUT

1½–2½ cups (375–625 ml) pure olive oil (don't use top-quality oil)

1½–2½ cups (375–625 ml) grapeseed or canola oil

2 large fresh rosemary sprigs

5 cloves garlic, coarsely chopped

2 large chipotle chiles, stemmed, seeded, and thinly sliced crosswise

Salt and freshly ground pepper

4 halibut fillets, 5–6 oz (155–185 g) each

2 heads frisée, pale inner leaves only, cut into bite-size pieces

Flaky sea salt, such as Maldon, for serving

serves 4

Noodle Bowl with Soy-Glazed Duck, Shiitake Mushrooms & Winter Greens

A soup takes the chill off of any winter day. Here, a highly seasoned broth is laced with wilted Tuscan kale leaves, roasted shiitakes, noodles, and roast duck just before serving. Seek out the dark soy sauce at an Asian market to add umami flavor.

8 cups (2 l) chicken broth

1-inch (2.5-cm) piece fresh ginger, peeled

2-inch (5-cm) piece lemongrass, white part only

1 tbsp plus 1 tsp fish sauce

3 tbsp soy sauce

Chile paste

4 green onions, white and pale green parts sliced paper-thin, dark green parts chopped for garnish

½ lb (250 g) shiitake mushrooms, brushed clean, stemmed, and caps cut into bite-size pieces

Nonstick cooking spray

Salt

¾ lb (375 g) boneless, skin-on duck breasts

2 tbsp dark soy sauce

2 tbsp mirin or medium-dry sherry

3 oz (90 g) cellophane (bean thread) noodles

2–3 oz (60–90 g) bok choy and Tuscan kale and/or other winter greens, such as chard or spinach, tough stems removed and leaves cut crosswise into ¼-inch (6-mm) strips

serves 4–6

In a saucepan, combine the broth, ginger, and lemongrass. Bring to a simmer over medium heat, then reduce the heat and simmer for 15 minutes. Remove and discard the ginger. Remove the lemongrass and mince, then return to the broth. Stir in the fish sauce, 1 tbsp of the soy sauce, chile paste to taste, and sliced green onions. Cover and set aside.

Preheat the oven to 475°F (245°C). Line a rimmed baking sheet with aluminum foil.

Spread the mushrooms in a single layer on the prepared baking sheet. Coat them lightly with nonstick cooking spray and season lightly with salt. Place a flat rack over the mushrooms and place the duck breasts, skin side up, on the rack. In a small bowl, whisk together the remaining 2 tbsp soy sauce and mirin and brush the mixture over the duck skin. Roast, brushing the duck every 3 minutes or so with the glaze, until the skin is glossy and dark and an instant-read thermometer inserted into the thickest part of the meat registers 130°F (54°C), 15–18 minutes. Transfer the duck to a cutting board and, when cool enough to handle, cut crosswise into slices ¼ inch (6 mm) thick.

Meanwhile, place the noodles in a bowl, cover with hot water, and let stand until softened, about 5 minutes. Drain and set aside.

Return the broth to a simmer over medium-low heat. Add the greens and cook until just tender but still bright green, 5–8 minutes, depending on the type of greens. Add the noodles and mushrooms and cook for 2 minutes longer.

Ladle the broth and vegetables into warmed bowls and top with the duck. Sprinkle with the chopped green onions and serve.

ADD SEASONAL EMBELLISHMENT

The best bowls are a synchronized display of seasonal ingredients. For extra color and flavor, try adding sliced kumquats, shaved radish, or julienned carrot.

Beef Tenderloin with Celery Root–Potato Purée

The look of celery root, which lands in markets in late fall and remains into spring, can be off-putting. But take a sturdy paring knife to its knobby, tough exterior and you'll discover smooth ivory flesh with a mild celery flavor.

1 beef tenderloin, about 3½ lb (1.75 kg)

9 tbsp (4½ oz/140 g) unsalted butter

Kosher salt

1–2 tsp coarsely cracked peppercorns

2 lb (1 kg) Yukon gold potatoes, peeled and cut into 1-inch (2.5 cm) pieces

1 celery root, peeled and cut into 1-inch (2.5-cm) pieces

Salt

¼ cup (60 ml) half-and-half, heated

2 tsp fresh lemon juice

Freshly ground white pepper

Chopped fresh flat-leaf parsley for garnish

serves 6–8

If the beef tenderloin roast has a skinny end, fold it under and tie it with kitchen string to create a uniform diameter. Pat the roast dry with paper towels and place on a rack set over a rimmed baking sheet. Melt 4 tbsp of the butter and brush all over the roast. Season generously with salt and cracked peppercorns, pressing gently to help the seasoning adhere. Let stand at room temperature for 30–60 minutes.

Preheat the oven to 450°F (230°C).

Roast the beef until an instant-read thermometer inserted into the thickest part registers 115°F (46°C) for rare, or 125°F (52°C) for medium-rare. Start checking the temperature after 20 minutes of roasting. Transfer the beef to a cutting board, tent with aluminum foil, and let rest for 10 minutes.

Meanwhile, in a large saucepan, combine the potatoes, celery root, 2 tsp salt, and water to cover by 2 inches (5 cm). Bring to a boil over high heat, then reduce the heat to medium and cook until the vegetables are tender, about 20 minutes. Drain, return the vegetables to the saucepan, and mash with a potato masher (or transfer to a food processor and pulse) until the mixture is smooth. Add the remaining 5 tbsp butter and the half-and-half and whisk (or pulse) until blended. Stir in the lemon juice and season to taste with salt and white pepper. Keep the purée warm until ready to serve.

Cut the beef into thick slices, reserving any accumulated juices. Spoon a dollop of the purée onto individual plates and arrange the beef on top. Spoon any juices over the meat, sprinkle with parsley, and serve.

Five-Spice Pork Loin with Mango, Green Onion & Mint Salsa

Most commercial pork is very lean and will benefit from about 6 hours in a simple brine (see page 78). If possible, buy a pork loin from a heritage breed, such as Berkshire or Duroc, which will have more marbling and thus better flavor.

Line a roasting pan with aluminum foil and place a flat wire rack inside the pan.

In a small saucepan, combine the mirin and marmalade. Bring just to a simmer over medium heat, stirring occasionally, then remove from the heat. Stir in the five-spice powder and salt. Place the pork on the rack in the prepared roasting pan and brush on all sides with some of the five-spice glaze. Cover loosely with plastic wrap and let stand at room temperature for about 1 hour, brushing once or twice with more glaze.

Preheat the oven to 400°F (200°C). Brush the pork with a little more glaze. Roast for 20 minutes, then reduce the oven temperature to 325°F (165°C). Continue to roast, basting occasionally with the glaze, until the exterior is glossy and golden brown and an instant-read thermometer inserted into the thickest part of the meat registers 150°F (65°C), 25–35 minutes longer. (The timing will depend on the diameter, not on the weight, of the roast; a roast with a larger diameter will take longer.)

To make the salsa, in a nonreactive bowl, combine the mango, bell pepper, jalapeño, green onions, mint, lime juice, and salt. Toss gently and let stand at room temperature for about 15 minutes or up to 1 hour (any longer and the mango will become mushy).

Remove the pork from the oven, tent with aluminum foil, and let rest on the rack for 5–10 minutes. Transfer the pork to a cutting board and cut into slices about ½ inch (12 mm) thick. Serve on warmed plates with the salsa on the side.

¼ cup (60 ml) mirin

¼ cup (2½ oz/75 g) orange marmalade or apricot jam

1 tbsp five-spice powder

1 tsp salt

1 boneless pork loin, 3½–4 lb (1.75–2 kg), excess fat trimmed

FOR THE SALSA

1 large or 2 small mangoes, pitted, peeled, and diced

1 small red bell pepper, seeded and diced

1 jalapeño chile, seeded and minced

5 green onions, finely chopped

2 tbsp finely chopped fresh mint

1½ tbsp fresh lime juice

¼–½ tsp salt

serves 6–8

Rack of Lamb with Spicy Cranberry Relish

This zesty take on the ubiquitous holiday-table cranberry relish adds both a jolt of chile heat and a dose of cool fresh mint. Change up the centerpiece on your menu, too, by serving this easy rack of lamb in place of the usual bird.

In a large, shallow dish, combine the tangerine juice and canola oil and season with salt and pepper. Add the lamb and turn to coat the racks on all sides. Let stand at room temperature for about 1 hour, turning occasionally.

Meanwhile, make the relish: Juice 1 of the tangerines and coarsely chop the other, peel and all, discarding any seeds. In a food processor, combine the tangerine juice, chopped tangerine, cranberries, onion, vinegar, mint, and jalapeño and pulse until finely chopped but still chunky. Pour the mixture into a bowl and stir in sugar to taste and the salt. Let stand at room temperature for at least 30 minutes or up to 2 hours.

Preheat the oven to 450°F (230°C).

If desired, wrap the ends of the lamb bones with aluminum foil to keep them from burning. Arrange the lamb racks, bone side down, in a roasting pan. Roast until an instant-read thermometer inserted into the center of the lamb, away from the bone, registers 130°F (54°C) for medium-rare, 15–20 minutes, or until done to your liking. Transfer the racks to a carving board, tent with aluminum foil, and let rest for 10–15 minutes.

Cut the racks between the bones into individual chops. Arrange 2 or 3 chops per person on warmed individual plates, spoon the relish alongside, and serve.

½ cup (125 ml) fresh tangerine juice

¼ cup (60 ml) canola or grapeseed oil

Salt and freshly ground pepper

3 racks of lamb, about 2½ lb (1.25 kg) each, trimmed and frenched

FOR THE RELISH

2 tangerines

1 cup (4 oz/125 g) fresh or frozen cranberries

½ large white onion, coarsely chopped

⅓ cup (80 ml) rice vinegar

¼ cup (¼ oz/7 g) packed fresh mint leaves

1 small jalapeño chile, coarsely chopped

3 tbsp sugar, or to taste

Pinch of salt

serves 8–10

Salted Caramel–Dipped Pears

Select a good eating-out-of-hand pear, such as Red Bartlett, Forelle, or Comice, for this irresistible fruit dessert with a toffee-like glaze. Make sure each fruit has a long stem, so your fingers stay clear of the superhot caramel when dipping.

4 ripe pears, preferably with long stems

Black lava salt and/or flaky sea salt, such as Maldon

1⅓ cups (10 oz/315 g) granulated sugar

1 tsp kosher salt

1¼ cups (310 ml) heavy cream

Dulce de leche ice cream for serving

serves 4 —

Refrigerate the pears for at least 2 hours. Cut a sliver from the base of the pears so they will stand upright. Place some lava salt on a small plate next to the stove top where you will be cooking the caramel. Line a baking sheet with lightly greased parchment paper or waxed paper and place near the stove top.

In a small, heavy saucepan, combine the sugar and salt with ½ cup (125 ml) water. Stir over low heat until the sugar is dissolved, then bring to a simmer over medium-high heat. Simmer briskly, watching carefully and without stirring, until the syrup turns a medium golden brown, 7–9 minutes. Immediately add the cream (watch out, it will splatter) and continue to simmer briskly, swirling the pan occasionally, until the mixture reaches 240°F (116°C) on a candy thermometer. Pour the caramel into a metal bowl to stop the cooking.

Remove the pan from the heat and immediately coat the pears: Holding a pear by its stem, dip the pear into the caramel, tipping the pan and rolling the pear around so that the caramel reaches to within about 1 inch (2.5 cm) of the stem. Let the excess caramel drip back into the pan, then place the pear upright on the prepared baking sheet. Repeat with the remaining pears. Let stand until the coating sets, about 10 minutes.

Serve each pear with a scoop of dulce de leche ice cream on the side. Serve the pears within 24 hours of coating, or the caramel will begin to weep.

SUMPTUOUS PRESENTATION
Use pears that are tender and fully
ripe, then serve them with a full set
of dessert flatware—fork and knife for
the fruit, and spoon for the ice cream.

Walnut Torte with Chocolate-Caramel Sauce

Italian nut tortes are popular throughout Italy and commonly feature almonds, hazelnuts, pistachios, or walnuts, as in this recipe. A dusting of cocoa powder and an orange-scented caramel sauce add an elegant touch, but use the sauce sparingly.

FOR THE CAKE

4 tbsp (2 oz/60 g) unsalted butter, melted and slightly cooled

2½ cups (10 oz/315 g) walnut halves

4 large eggs, separated, at room temperature

1 cup (8 oz/250 g) granulated sugar

Pinch of salt

FOR THE SAUCE

¼ cup (2 oz/60 g) plus 2 tbsp firmly packed golden brown sugar

⅓ cup (80 ml) heavy cream

5 tbsp (2½ oz/75 g) butter

⅓ cup (2 oz/60 g) semisweet chocolate chips

Cocoa powder for dusting

Confectioners' sugar for dusting

makes one 9-inch (23-cm) cake; serves 10–12

To make the cake, preheat the oven to 325°F (165°C). Generously coat a 9-inch (23-cm) springform pan with 1 tbsp of the melted butter. Line the bottom with parchment paper and butter the parchment. Reserve the remaining butter.

Using a nut grinder, a rotary cheese grater with small holes, or the small holes of a box grater, finely grind or grate the walnuts. (Don't use a food processor or the nuts will be too heavy.) Gently scoop into a bowl. Set aside.

In a bowl, using an electric mixer, beat the egg yolks and ¾ cup (6 oz/185 g) of the granulated sugar on high speed until thickened and pale. Drizzle in the remaining butter and beat until combined.

In a clean bowl, using a clean whisk attachment, beat the egg whites and salt on low speed until foamy. Raise the speed to high and beat until peaks begin to form. Gradually add the remaining ¼ cup (2 oz/60 g) granulated sugar and beat until the whites hold stiff, glossy peaks.

Scoop about one-third of the whites into the bowl with the yolk mixture. Sprinkle one-third of the walnuts over the top and gently fold together. Fold in another one-third of the whites and walnuts, then fold in the rest until no white streaks remain. Scrape the batter into the prepared pan.

Bake until the top is nicely browned and a cake tester inserted into the center comes out clean, about 45 minutes. Let cool in the pan on a wire rack for 20 minutes. Run a knife around the inside edge of the pan. Remove the ring from the pan and let the cake cool to room temperature.

To make the chocolate caramel sauce, in a saucepan, combine the brown sugar, cream, and butter. Place over medium heat and bring to a boil, stirring constantly. Add the chocolate chips and cook, stirring, until melted and smooth, about 2 minutes.

To serve, carefully invert the cake onto a plate and gently remove the metal bottom. Peel off the parchment. Invert the cake onto a serving platter. Dust with cocoa powder and confectioners' sugar and serve with the sauce.

Pink Grapefruit Sorbet with Crystallized Ginger

Grapefruits have a yellow peel, sometimes with a bit of blush, and flesh that ranges from white to pink to red. To give your sorbet a vibrant hue, look for such varieties as Star Ruby, Ruby Red, or, for the deepest color, Flame for juicing.

In a saucepan, combine the the sugar, zest, salt and 1½ cups (375 ml) water over medium-high heat and heat, stirring until the sugar is completely dissolved, 3–4 minutes. Let cool completely. Strain the resulting sugar syrup into a bowl and discard the zest. Stir in the grapefruit juice. Cover the bowl with plastic wrap and refrigerate until the sorbet mixture is very cold, at least 3 hours or up to 8 hours.

Prepare an ice cream maker with at least a 1-qt (1-l) capacity according to the manufacturer's directions. Remove the plastic wrap from the bowl, pour the sorbet mixture into the ice cream maker, and churn until it has thickened and mounds on the paddle.

The sorbet can be served right away, but for a fuller flavor and a firmer consistency, transfer the sorbet to a plastic freezer container, cover tightly, and freeze until firm, at least 3 hours or up to 2 days. Sprinkle with the crystallized ginger pieces before serving.

1 cup (8 oz/250 g) sugar

1 tbsp freshly grated red grapefruit zest

Pinch of salt

1½ cups (375 ml) fresh red grapefruit juice, seeds and pulp strained

⅓ cup (2 oz/60 g) chopped crystallized ginger

serves 6

Crème Brûlée with Caramelized Blood Oranges

The best crème brûlée marries a thick layer of velvety vanilla custard with a brittle burnt-sugar crust. To ensure the base is rich, creamy, and still trembles slightly when cooked, egg yolks rather than whole eggs are used.

3 cups (750 ml) heavy cream

½ cup (4 oz/125 g) granulated sugar

⅛ tsp salt

1 vanilla bean

8 large egg yolks

FOR THE BLOOD ORANGES

2 blood oranges, preferably Moro

¼ cup (2 oz/60 g) granulated sugar

6–8 tsp turbinado sugar

makes 6–8 crèmes brûlées

Preheat the oven to 300°F (150°C). Have ready 6–8 shallow ramekins or custard cups, each ½–1 cup (125–250 ml), and a large baking pan to hold all the cups.

In a saucepan, stir together the cream, granulated sugar, and salt. Split the vanilla bean lengthwise and scrape out the seeds. Add the seeds and pod to the cream, place over medium heat, and bring to a very gentle boil, stirring constantly. Remove from the heat, cover, and let stand for 20 minutes.

Meanwhile, in a bowl, whisk the egg yolks just to break them up. Whisking constantly, slowly add the cream mixture. Pour the yolk mixture through a fine-mesh sieve into a pitcher, then divide among the ramekins. Place the ramekins in the baking pan, place the baking pan on the oven rack, and carefully pour hot water into the pan to reach about halfway up the sides of the ramekins. Bake until the custards are just set but still jiggly, 30–35 minutes.

Remove the custards from the water bath and let cool completely on a wire rack. Cover with plastic wrap pressed directly onto the surface of the custards to prevent a skin from forming. Refrigerate at least 2 hours or up to 2 days.

To prepare the blood oranges, use a serrated knife to slice off both ends of each orange. Working with 1 fruit at a time, stand it upright and, following the contour of the fruit, carefully slice downward to remove the peel, pith, and membrane. Set the fruit on its side and cut crosswise into thin slices, discarding any seeds.

In a saucepan, stir together the granulated sugar and 2 tbsp water. Place over medium-high heat and cook, swirling the pan occasionally, until the syrup turns a deep amber caramel. Immediately remove from the heat, add the orange slices, and swirl the pan to coat them evenly.

Just before serving, preheat the broiler. Sprinkle each custard with a thin, even layer of 1 tsp of the turbinado sugar. Place on a baking sheet and broil until the sugar caramelizes. Watch carefully so the custards do not burn. (Alternatively, caramelize the sugar with a kitchen torch.) Set the custards aside to harden for a few minutes, then top with the caramelized oranges and serve.

SPARKLING CITRUS
Any variety of orange
will work in this recipe.
For the most striking
color, look for Moro
variety blood oranges,
which are prized for
their intensely scarlet,
sweet flesh.

A Cocktail for Every Season

Mint Mojito

8 sprigs fresh mint, plus 1 sprig for garnish

Splash of simple syrup

1 oz (30 ml) fresh lime juice

2 oz (60 ml) golden or white rum

Fill a highball glass with ice. In a cocktail shaker, muddle the mint sprigs with the simple syrup, lime juice, and ice. Add the rum and shake well. Strain into the prepared glass. Garnish with the remaining mint sprig.

Blackberry Martini

2 tbsp blackberries, plus more for garnish

½ oz (15 ml) simple syrup

2 oz (60 ml) vodka or gin

½ oz (15 ml) crème de cassis

In a cocktail shaker, muddle the blackberries with the simple syrup and ice. Add the vodka and crème de cassis and shake well. Strain into a martini glass. Garnish with blackberries.

The best cocktail garnishes do double duty, delivering both flavor and eye appeal. Everyone is familiar with the citrus twist, jarred cherry, or olive—along with the pretty little umbrella—so here are four new ideas that are not only seasonal but also taste and look good.

The Hayride

1 lemon wedge and cinnamon sugar for rim

2 oz (60 ml) bourbon

½ oz (15 ml) pear brandy

2 oz (60 ml) spiced cider

Pear slice for garnish

Moisten the rim of a lowball glass with lemon, then dip in cinnamon sugar. Fill the glass with ice. In a cocktail shaker, shake the bourbon, brandy, and cider with ice. Strain into the prepared glass. Garnish with a pear slice.

Cranberry Daiquiri

1½ tbsp Drunken Cranberries (page 167), plus 1 oz (30 ml) of their liquid

2 oz (60 ml) dark rum

1 oz (30 ml) fresh lime juice

Fill a martini glass with crushed ice. Add 1 tbsp of the cranberries. In a cocktail shaker, shake the cranberry liquid, rum, and lime juice with ice. Strain into the prepared glass. Garnish with the remaining cranberries.

Produce in Season

Not sure when your favorite fruits and vegetables are in season? Use these lists to find out—and choose fresh ingredients at their prime.

SPRING

FRUITS

avocados
blackberries
black currants
blood oranges
blueberries
dried currants
fraises des bois
grapefruits
kiwifruits
kumquats
lemons
limes
mangoes
Meyer lemons
navel oranges
papayas
pears
pineapples
prunes
raisins
raspberries
red currants
rhubarb
strawberries

VEGETABLES

arugula
asaparagus
artichokes
broccoli
broccoli rabe
butter lettuce
cabbage
carrots
cauliflower

celery
celery root
chanterelle mushrooms
chicories
endive
English peas
fava beans
fennel
fingerling potatoes
green beans
green bell peppers
green garlic
green onions
haricots verts
jicama
leeks
mâche
morel mushrooms
new potatoes
parsnips
pea shoots
purslane
radishes
rhubarb
shallots
shiitake mushrooms
snow peas
sorrel
spinach
spring onions
sugar snap peas
sweet onions
Swiss chard
watercress

SUMMER

FRUITS

apricots
avocados
blackberries
black currants
blueberries
cantaloupes
cherries
dates
figs
green mangoes
huckleberries
honeydew melons
limes
mangoes
nectarines
papayas
passion fruits
peaches
pineapples
plums
pluots
raspberries
strawberries
tomatillos
tomatoes
Valencia oranges
watermelons

VEGETABLES

arugula
beets
beet greens
bell peppers
carrots

chile peppers
corn
cranberry beans
cucumbers
eggplant
fingerling potatoes
garlic
green beans
haricots verts
Italian (romano) beans
lettuce
new potatoes
okra
onions
Padrón peppers
pea shoots
purslane
radishes
russet potatoes
shell beans
snow peas
sorrel
sugar snap peas
summer squashes
squash blossoms
sweet onions
tomatoes
wax beans
zucchini
zucchini flowers

FALL

FRUITS

apples
Asian pears
crab apples
cranberries
dates
dried fruits
figs
grapes
olives
pears
persimmons
plums
pomegranates
prunes
quinces

VEGETABLES

artichokes
arugula
avocados
beet greens
beets
black trumpet mushrooms
bok choy
broccoli
broccoli rabe
butternut squashes
cabbage
carrots
chard
chicory
chile peppers
collard greens
Delicata squashes
eggplants
endive
escarole
fennel
frisée
grapes
hedgehog mushrooms
horseradish
Jerusalem artichokes
kabocha squash
kale
kohlrabi
leeks
onions
parsnips
porcini mushrooms
potatoes
pumpkins
radicchio
radishes
red-leaf lettuce
red sorrel
Romanesco broccoli
rutabagas
shallots
shell beans
shiitake mushrooms
spinach
sweet potatoes
tomatoes
truffles
turnips
watercress

WINTER

FRUITS

apples
Asian pears
bananas
blood oranges
clementines
cranberries
dried fruits
grapefruits
kumquats
lemons
mandarins
navel oranges
olives
pears
persimmons
pomegranates
pomelos
prunes
raisins
tangerines

VEGETABLES

acorn squash
beets
bok choy
broccoli
broccoli rabe
brussels sprouts
butternut squash
cabbage
carrots
cauliflower
celery
celery root
chard
chicories
collard greens
Delicata squashes
dried mushrooms
endive
fennel
frisee
horseradish
Jerusalem artichokes
kale
kohlrabi
leeks
onions
parsnips
potatoes
pumpkins
red cabbage
Romanesco broccoli
rutabagas
shallots
snow peas
spinach
sweet potatoes
turnips
watercress

BASIC RECIPES

Thin-Crust Dough

makes two 9-oz (280-g) dough balls

1¼ cups (5½ oz/160 g) bread flour, plus more for dusting
1¼ cups (5½ oz/160 g) all-purpose flour
1 tsp salt
1 cup (250 ml) warm water (110°–115°F/43°–46°C)
¾ tsp active dry yeast
1½ tsp olive oil, plus more for the bowl

In a large bowl, combine both flours and the salt. In a glass measuring cup, stir together the water, yeast, and olive oil and pour into the flour mixture. Using lightly floured hands, knead until well combined and springy, about 3 minutes, scraping the sides of the bowl as needed. Cover the bowl with plastic wrap and let rest at room temperature for 20 minutes. Turn the dough out onto a lightly floured surface and knead until smooth, about 3 minutes. Shape the dough into a ball. Place in an oiled clean bowl and cover with plastic wrap or a damp kitchen towel. Let rise at room temperature for 4½–5 hours, or in the refrigerator for 8–24 hours; bring refrigerated dough to room temperature for 45–60 minutes before continuing. Shape the dough into 2 balls. Note: This dough freezes well. After letting it rise, wrap 1 or both dough balls in plastic wrap and freeze for up to 6 months; bring to room temperature for about 4 hours before shaping.

Flaky Pie Dough

makes one 9-inch (23-cm) pie or tart crust, or 4 potpie crusts

1¼ cups (6½ oz/200 g) all-purpose flour
¼ tsp salt
½ tsp sugar (optional)
7 tbsp (3½ oz/105 g) very cold unsalted butter, cut into cubes
5 tbsp (80 ml) ice water, plus more as needed

In a food processor, combine the flour, salt, and sugar (if using), and pulse to mix. Sprinkle the butter over the top and pulse for a few seconds, just until the butter is slightly broken up into the flour but still in visible pieces. Evenly sprinkle the water over the flour mixture, then process just until the mixture starts to come together (add a little more water, if needed). Dump the dough into a large lock-top plastic bag and press into a flat disk. Refrigerate for at least 30 minutes or up to 1 day, or freeze for up to 1 month.

Almond Tart Dough

makes 1 lb (500 g) dough

⅓ cup (1½ oz/45 g) raw whole almonds
1⅔ cups (7 oz/200 g) all-purpose flour, plus more for dusting
Pinch of salt
½ cup (4 oz/125 g) plus 1 tbsp very cold unsalted butter, cut into small cubes
3 tbsp cold fresh orange juice
2–3 tbsp cold water

In a food processor, grind the almonds to a fine, grainy powder. Add the flour and salt and pulse to mix. Add the butter and pulse in 2-second intervals, 4 or 5 times, just until the mixture resembles large bread crumbs. Drizzle the orange juice and 2 tbsp of the water evenly over the flour mixture and pulse just until the dough begins to clump together and form a rough, shaggy mass, adding the remaining 1 tablespoon water if needed; do not overwork.

Transfer the dough to a lightly floured surface, gather into a ball, and shape into a disk. Wrap with plastic wrap and refrigerate for at least 2 hours or up to overnight. Let stand at room temperature for 20–30 minutes before rolling out.

Tomato Sauce

makes about 3 cups (750 ml)

¾ lb (12 oz/375 g) firm-ripe heirloom tomatoes
1½ tbsp extra-virgin olive oil
½ small white or yellow onion, finely chopped
2 tsp tomato paste
1 tsp fresh lemon juice
⅛ tsp Sriracha or other hot sauce
Fine sea salt and freshly ground pepper
2 tsp coarsely chopped fresh basil

Bring a saucepan of water to a boil and fill another bowl with ice water. Cut a shallow X in the base of each tomato. Blanch the tomatoes for 20 seconds. Transfer to the ice water to stop the cooking. Core the tomatoes, then slip off and discard the skins. Cut in half crosswise and squeeze out the seeds and excess liquid. Cut the tomatoes into small dice. In the saucepan, warm the olive oil over medium-high heat. Add the onion and stir occasionally until softened, about 4 minutes. Add the tomato paste and stir for 1 minute, then add the chopped tomatoes, lemon juice, Sriracha, ½ teaspoon salt, and plenty of pepper. Simmer over medium-low heat, stirring occasionally, until thickened slightly, 8–12 minutes. Remove from the heat and stir in the basil.

Chanterelle Ragout

serves 6–8

2 tbsp unsalted butter

1 tbsp olive oil

2 large shallots, finely chopped

2 lb (1 kg) chanterelles or other wild or cultivated mushrooms, such as cremini or shiitake, brushed clean, tough stems trimmed, and caps cut into bite-size pieces

3 cloves garlic, minced

5 fresh thyme sprigs

⅓ cup (80 ml) fortified or dessert wine, preferably Madeira

Salt and freshly ground pepper

⅓ cup (3 oz/90 g) crème fraîche

¼ cup (⅓ oz/10 g) coarsely chopped flat-leaf parsley

In a large sauté pan over medium heat, melt the butter with the olive oil. Add the shallots and cook, stirring occasionally, until beginning to soften, about 4 minutes. Add the mushrooms and cook, stirring occasionally, until softened and almost dry, about 7 minutes. Add the garlic and thyme and cook, stirring occasionally, until fragrant, about 1 minute. Add the wine and ½ tsp salt and simmer until most of the liquid is evaporated, about 3 minutes. Stir in the crème fraîche and parsley and simmer until very thick, 2–3 minutes. Discard the thyme sprigs. Season with salt and pepper.

Carrot-Apple Purée

makes about 2 cups (16 oz/500 g)

2 large carrots, peeled and cut into ¾-inch (2-cm) dice

2 large yellow or green apples, peeled, cored, and cut into ¾-inch (2-cm) dice

1 cup (250 ml) heavy cream

In a steamer basket set over a large saucepan of simmering water, steam the carrots and apples until tender, 10–12 minutes. Transfer to a food processor, add the cream, and purée until smooth. Season lightly with salt and pepper and pulse to mix.

Pumpkin Purée

makes about 1 cup (8 oz/250 g)

1 Sugar pumpkin

Preheat the oven to 325°F (160°C). Cut the pumpkin in half and remove the seeds and ribs. Place in a roasting pan, cover with aluminum foil, and roast until tender, about 1 hour. Let cool, then purée in a food processor.

Drunken Cranberries

makes about 3 cups (750 ml)

1½ cups (375 ml) simple syrup

2 cinnamon sticks

Grated zest from 1 large orange

1 cup (4 oz/125 g) fresh cranberries

1½ cups (375 ml) white rum

In a large saucepan, combine the simple syrup, cinnamon sticks, and the orange zest. Bring to a boil over medium-high heat and add the cranberries. Cook until the cranberries just begin to pop, about 1 minute. Remove from the heat and let cool slightly, then strain the liquid into a large glass jar. Add the cranberries to the jar (discarding the cinnamon and orange zest), then add the rum. If the cranberries are not fully submerged in the liquid, add equal parts simple syrup and rum until they are covered. Let cool, then cover and refrigerate for at least 2 hours or up to 3 weeks.

INDEX

A

Aioli, Spicy Garlic, 60
Almonds
    Almond Tart Dough, 166
    Rhubarb-Ginger Crumble with
        Cardamom Cream, 47
    Romaine & Roasted Delicata Squash
        Salad with Dates, Almonds
        & Bacon, 100
Apples
    Apple Fritters with Cinnamon
        Cream, 117
    Carrot-Apple Purée, 167
    Pear, Quince & Apple Galette, 119
    Pork Skewers with Apple, Fresh Sage
        & Rustic Bread, 108
Apricots
    Apricot Pistachio Tart, 82
    Stone Fruit Salad with Summer
        Lettuces, Hazelnuts
        & Goat Cheese, 68
Artichoke, Celery & Fennel Salad, 29
Arugula
    Arugula Pesto, 37
    Fuyu Persimmon Salad with
        Endive & Pomegranate, 142
    Peach Flatbread with Burrata,
        Arugula & Pickled Onion, 56
Asparagus
    Orecchiette with Spring Vegetables,
        Pecorino & Prosciutto, 31
    Sesame-Ginger Noodles with Peas,
        Shaved Asparagus & Radishes, 39
    Stir-Fried Beef with Asparagus, Bok
        Choy & Morels, 42
Avocados
    Avocado Crema, 76
    Grilled Rib-Eye Steak with
        Avocado Chimichurri, 71
    Soft Tacos with Pumpkin, Black Beans
        & Avocado, 101
    Summer Vegetable Ceviche, 55

B

Bacon & pancetta
    Creamy Cauliflower Soup with
        Brussels Sprout Hash, 130
    Pizza with Roasted Broccolini,
        Pancetta & Pine Nuts, 145
    Pork Skewers with Apple, Fresh Sage
        & Rustic Bread, 106
    Potato & Pancetta Crostata with
        Fresh Rosemary, 133
    Romaine & Roasted Delicata Squash
        Salad with Dates, Almonds
        & Bacon, 100

Basic recipes
    Almond Tart Dough, 166
    Carrot-Apple Purée, 167
    Chanterelle Ragout, 167
    Drunken Cranberries, 167
    Flaky Pie Dough, 166
    Pumpkin Purée, 167
    Thin-Crust Dough, 166
    Tomato Sauce, 166–67
Beans
    Chicken Tagine with Roasted Squash,
        Haricots Verts, Chickpeas
        & Cranberries, 106
    fava, about, 34
    Fresh Spring Rolls with Crab, Mango,
        Jicama & Haricots Verts, 24
    Green Bean + Cherry Tomato
        Salad, 122
    Kale, White Bean & Sausage Soup, 97
    Pan-Seared Halloumi with Fava Beans,
        Mint & Lemon, 21
    Pan-Seared Salmon with Fresh Favas
        & Arugula Pesto, 37
    Soft Tacos with Pumpkin, Black Beans
        & Avocado, 101
    Types of, 34–35
Beef
    Beef Tenderloin with Celery Root–
        Potato Purée, 150
    Grilled Rib-Eye Steak with
        Avocado Chimichurri, 71
    Short Ribs with Carrot-Apple
        Purée, 110
    Stir-Fried Beef with Asparagus,
        Bok Choy & Morels, 42
    Thai Beef Salad with Cucumber, Chile
        & Greens, 63
Beets, Roasted Red & Yellow,
    with Burrata, Sherry Vinaigrette
    & Escarole, 127
Blackberry & Blueberry Potpies, 81
Blackberry Martini, 161
Black Lentil Salad with Shrimp,
    Green Garlic, Snap Peas
    & Moroccan Vinaigrette, 28
Blistered Padrón Peppers with
    Spicy Garlic Aioli, 60
Blueberry & Blackberry Potpies, 81
Bok Choy, Asparagus & Morels,
    Stir-Fried Beef with, 42
Breads
    Cumin-Crusted Pita Chips, 93
    Peach Flatbread with Burrata,
        Arugula & Pickled Onion, 56
    A Toast for Every Season, 50–51
    Torn Croutons, 61

Broccolini, Pancetta & Pine Nuts,
    Pizza with, 145
Brussels sprouts
    Creamy Cauliflower Soup with
        Brussels Sprout Hash, 130
    Mushroom + Brussels Sprout
        Salad, 123
    Pasta with Brussels Sprout Leaves,
        Hazelnuts & Brown Butter, 146

C

Cabbage, Red, & Carrot Slaw, 105
Cake, Naked Carrot, with Spring
    Blossoms, 48
Caper-Olive Gremolata, 99
Cardamom Cream, 47
Carrots
    Carrot-Apple Purée, 167
    Little Gem Salad with Shaved
        Carrot, Sunflower Seeds
        & Dill Vinaigrette, 26
    Naked Carrot Cake with
        Spring Blossoms, 48
    Red Cabbage & Carrot Slaw, 105
    Rice-Noodle Salad with Chicken,
        Summer Vegetables & Herbs, 66
Cauliflower
    Creamy Cauliflower Soup with
        Brussels Sprout Hash, 130
    Seared Cauliflower Steaks with
        Olive-Caper Gremolata, 99
Celery
    Artichoke, Celery & Fennel Salad, 29
    Mixed Citrus Salad with Mâche,
        Fennel & Celery, 140
Celery Root–Potato Purée,
    Beef Tenderloin with, 150
Chanterelle Ragout, 167
Cheese
    Creamy Parmesan Polenta with
        Wild Mushrooms, 91
    Fig, Blue Cheese & Walnut Crostini
        with Honey Drizzle, 92
    Fried Squash Blossoms with
        Ricotta, 57
    Heirloom Tomato Tart, 58
    Mushroom + Sage Toast, 51
    Orecchiette with Spring Vegetables,
        Pecorino & Prosciutto, 31
    Oven-Roasted Ricotta with
        Citrus & Pomegranate, 132
    Pan-Seared Halloumi with
        Fava Beans, Mint & Lemon, 21
    Peach Flatbread with Burrata,
        Arugula & Pickled Onion, 56
    Pea + Radish Toast, 50

Pizza with Roasted Broccolini,
Pancetta & Pine Nuts, 145
Pomegranate + Walnut Toast, 51
Ricotta & Pea Crostini with
Tarragon & Pink Peppercorns, 20
Roasted Figs with Mascarpone, 121
Roasted Red & Yellow Beets
with Burrata, Sherry Vinaigrette
& Escarole, 127
Stone Fruit Salad with Summer
Lettuces, Hazelnuts
& Goat Cheese, 68
Tomato + Basil Toast, 50
Watermelon, Nectarine & Mint Salad
with Feta Cheese, 69
Watermelon Radish Salad with
Herbed Cheese, Blood Orange
& Chives, 18
Zucchini Lasagna with Herbed Ricotta
& Fresh Heirloom Tomato Sauce, 73
Cherry Clafoutis, Summer, 83
Chicken
Chicken Tagine with Roasted Squash,
Haricots Verts, Chickpeas
& Cranberries, 106
Cider-Braised Chicken Legs with
Fresh Figs & Cipollini Onions, 116
Honey-Glazed Chicken Thighs with
Rhubarb-Mint-Radish Slaw, 40
Pounded Chicken Breasts with
Grilled Ratatouille, 79
Rice-Noodle Salad with Chicken,
Summer Vegetables & Herbs, 66
Chile-Spiced Halibut with Frisée &
Tangerine Salad, 147
Chocolate-Caramel Sauce, 156
Cider-Braised Chicken Legs with
Fresh Figs & Cipollini Onions, 116
Cioppino, Crab, 139
Citrus Galette, 87
Clafoutis, Summer Cherry, 83
Clams
Clams in Leek Broth with
Parsley Vinaigrette, 25
Crab Cioppino, 139
Cocktails for Every Season, 160–61
Coconut-Curry Butternut Squash
Soup, 96
Corn
Farro, Grilled Corn & Summer Squash
Salad, 64
Heirloom Tomato Tart, 58
Risotto with Fresh Corn & Basil Oil, 65
Crab
Crab Cioppino, 139
Fresh Spring Rolls with Crab, Mango,
Jicama & Haricots Verts, 24

Cranberries
Chicken Tagine with Roasted Squash,
Haricots Verts, Chickpeas &
Cranberries, 106
Cranberry Daiquiri, 160
Drunken Cranberries, 167
Spicy Cranberry Relish, 153
Creamy Cauliflower Soup with
Brussels Sprout Hash, 130
Creamy Parmesan Polenta with
Wild Mushrooms, 91
Crème Brûlée with Caramelized
Blood Oranges, 158
Crostata, Potato & Pancetta,
with Fresh Rosemary, 133
Crostini
Crostini with Radicchio, Smoked Trout
& Horseradish Cream, 129
Fig, Blue Cheese & Walnut Crostini
with Honey Drizzle, 92
Ricotta & Pea Crostini with Tarragon
& Pink Peppercorns, 20
Cucumbers
Golden Gazpacho with Torn Croutons
& Cherry Tomato Salsa, 61
Rice-Noodle Salad with Chicken,
Summer Vegetables & Herbs, 66
Summer Vegetable Ceviche, 55
Thai Beef Salad with Cucumber,
Chile & Greens, 63
Curry-Coconut Butternut Squash
Soup, 96

D

Daiquiri, Cranberry, 160
Desserts
Apple Fritters with Cinnamon
Cream, 117
Apricot Pistachio Tart, 82
Blackberry & Blueberry Potpies, 81
Crème Brûlée with Caramelized
Blood Oranges, 158
A Galette for Every Season, 86–87
Kiwi & Passion Fruit Panna Cotta, 46
Naked Carrot Cake with Spring
Blossoms, 48
Pavlova with Meyer Lemon Curd
& Strawberries, 45
Pear, Quince & Apple Galette, 119
Pink Grapefruit Sorbet with
Crystallized Ginger, 157
Pumpkin Tart with
Gingersnap Crust, 120
Rhubarb-Ginger Crumble with
Cardamom Cream, 47
Roasted Figs with Mascarpone, 121
Salted Caramel–Dipped Pears, 154

Summer Cherry Clafoutis, 83
Walnut Torte with Chocolate-Caramel
Sauce, 156
Watermelon Mojito Pops, 84
Dips
Smoky Eggplant Dip with
Cumin-Crusted Pita Chips, 93
Spicy Garlic Aioli, 60
Duck, Soy-Glazed, Shiitake Mushrooms
& Winter Greens, Noodle Bowl
with, 148

E

Eggplant
Pounded Chicken Breasts with
Grilled Ratatouille, 79
Smoky Eggplant Dip with
Cumin-Crusted Pita Chips, 93
Eggs
Omelet-Soufflé with Spinach,
Leek & New Potatoes, 33
Swiss Chard & Spring Onion
Frittata, 32
Endive & Pomegranate, Fuyu Persimmon
Salad with, 142
English Pea & Watercress Soup, 23
Escarole, Burrata & Sherry Vinaigrette,
Roasted Red & Yellow Beets
with, 127

F

Farro, Grilled Corn & Summer Squash
Salad, 64
Fennel
Artichoke, Celery & Fennel Salad, 29
Mixed Citrus Salad with Mâche,
Fennel & Celery, 140
Figs
Cider-Braised Chicken Legs with
Fresh Figs & Cipollini Onions, 116
Fig, Blue Cheese & Walnut Crostini
with Honey Drizzle, 92
Roasted Figs with Mascarpone, 121
Fish
Chile-Spiced Halibut with Frisée
& Tangerine Salad, 147
Crab Cioppino, 139
Crostini with Radicchio, Smoked Trout
& Horseradish Cream, 129
Grilled Fish Tacos with Pineapple
Salsa & Avocado Crema, 76
Grilled Salmon with Stone Fruit–Herb
Mojo, 72
Pan-Seared Salmon with Fresh Favas
& Arugula Pesto, 37
Pan-Seared Sea Bass with
Acorn Squash, 113

Five-Spice Pork Loin with Mango, Green Onion & Mint Salsa, 151
Flaky Pie Dough, 166
Fresh Spring Rolls with Crab, Mango, Jicama & Haricots Verts, 24
Fried Squash Blossoms with Ricotta, 57
Frisée & Tangerine Salad, Chile-Spiced Halibut with, 147
Frittata, Swiss Chard & Spring Onion, 32
Fritters, Apple, with Cinnamon Cream, 117
Fruits. *See also specific fruits*
   fall and winter, 165
   spring, 164
   Stone Fruit Galette, 86
   Stone Fruit Salad with Summer Lettuces, Hazelnuts & Goat Cheese, 68
   summer, 74–75, 164
Fuyu Persimmon Salad with Endive & Pomegranate, 142

G

Galettes for Every Season, 86–87
Garlic Aioli, Spicy, 60
Ginger
   Pink Grapefruit Sorbet with Crystallized Ginger, 157
   Pumpkin Tart with Gingersnap Crust, 120
   Rhubarb-Ginger Crumble with Cardamom Cream, 47
Grains
   Creamy Parmesan Polenta with Wild Mushrooms, 91
   Risotto with Fresh Corn & Basil Oil, 65
   Wheat Berry Salad with Chopped Chard, Pear & Sunflower Seeds, 94
Grapefruit
   Citrus Galette, 87
   Pink Grapefruit Sorbet with Crystallized Ginger, 157
Green beans
   Chicken Tagine with Roasted Squash, Haricots Verts, Chickpeas & Cranberries, 106
   Fresh Spring Rolls with Crab, Mango, Jicama & Haricots Verts, 24
   Green Bean + Cherry Tomato Salad, 122
Greens
   Arugula Pesto, 37
   Chard + Squash Salad, 123
   Chile-Spiced Halibut with Frisée & Tangerine Salad, 147
   Crostini with Radicchio, Smoked Trout & Horseradish Cream, 129

English Pea & Watercress Soup, 23
Fuyu Persimmon Salad with Endive & Pomegranate, 142
Kale, White Bean & Sausage Soup, 97
Little Gem Salad with Shaved Carrot, Sunflower Seeds & Dill Vinaigrette, 26
Mixed Citrus Salad with Mâche, Fennel & Celery, 140
Noodle Bowl with Soy-Glazed Duck, Shiitake Mushrooms & Winter Greens, 148
Omelet-Soufflé with Spinach, Leek & New Potatoes, 33
Peach Flatbread with Burrata, Arugula & Pickled Onion, 56
Roasted Red & Yellow Beets with Burrata, Sherry Vinaigrette & Escarole, 127
Romaine & Roasted Delicata Squash Salad with Dates, Almonds & Bacon, 100
Stone Fruit Salad with Summer Lettuces, Hazelnuts & Goat Cheese, 68
Swiss Chard & Spring Onion Frittata, 32
Thai Beef Salad with Cucumber, Chile & Greens, 63
Warm Kale Salad with Lentils & Prosciutto, 143
Wheat Berry Salad with Chopped Chard, Pears & Sunflower Seeds, 94
Grilled Fish Tacos with Pineapple Salsa & Avocado Crema, 76
Grilled Lamb Chops with Spring Herb Pesto, 43
Grilled Pork Chops with Summer Plums & Thyme, 78
Grilled Rib-Eye Steak with Avocado Chimichurri, 71
Grilled Salmon with Stone Fruit–Herb Mojo, 72

H

Halibut, Chile-Spiced, with Frisée & Tangerine Salad, 147
Hayride, The, 160
Hazelnuts, Brussels Sprout Leaves & Brown Butter, Pasta with, 146
Heirloom Tomato Tart, 58
Herbs. *See also* Mint
   Grilled Rib-Eye Steak with Avocado Chimichurri, 71
   Mushroom + Sage Toast, 51
   Pork Skewers with Apple, Fresh Sage & Rustic Bread, 108
   Spring Herb Pesto, 43

Honey-Glazed Chicken Thighs with Rhubarb-Mint-Radish Slaw, 40

J

Jicama
   Fresh Spring Rolls with Crab, Mango, Jicama & Haricots Verts, 24
   Summer Vegetable Ceviche, 55
   Watermelon Radish Salad with Herbed Cheese, Blood Orange & Chives, 18

K

Kale
   Kale, White Bean & Sausage Soup, 97
   Warm Kale Salad with Lentils & Prosciutto, 143
Kiwi & Passion Fruit Panna Cotta, 46

L

Lamb
   Grilled Lamb Chops with Spring Herb Pesto, 43
   Rack of Lamb with Spicy Cranberry Relish, 153
Leek Broth, Clams in, with Parsley Vinaigrette, 25
Lemon, Meyer, Curd & Strawberries, Pavlova with, 45
Lentils
   Black Lentil Salad with Shrimp, Green Garlic, Snap Peas & Moroccan Vinaigrette, 28
   Warm Kale Salad with Lentils & Prosciutto, 143
Lettuce
   Little Gem Salad with Shaved Carrot, Sunflower Seeds & Dill Vinaigrette, 26
   Romaine & Roasted Delicata Squash Salad with Dates, Almonds & Bacon, 100
   Stone Fruit Salad with Summer Lettuces, Hazelnuts & Goat Cheese, 68
   Thai Beef Salad with Cucumber, Chile & Greens, 63

M

Mâche, Fennel & Celery, Mixed Citrus Salad with, 140
Mango
   Fresh Spring Rolls with Crab, Mango, Jicama & Haricots Verts, 24
   Mango, Green Onion & Mint Salsa, 151

Martini, Blackberry, 161
Mint
    Mint Mojito, 161
    Rhubarb-Mint-Radish Slaw, 40
    Spring Herb Pesto, 43
    Watermelon Mojito Pops, 84
Miso-Glazed Scallops, Seared, with
    Snow Peas & Green Garlic, 38
Mixed Citrus Salad with Mâche,
    Fennel & Celery, 140
Mojito, Mint, 161
Mushrooms
    Chanterelle Ragout, 167
    Creamy Parmesan Polenta with
        Wild Mushrooms, 91
    Mushroom + Brussels Sprout
        Salad, 123
    Mushroom + Sage Toast, 51
    Mushroom Soup with Crispy
        Prosciutto & Marjoram, 138
    Noodle Bowl with Soy-Glazed
        Duck, Shiitake Mushrooms
        & Winter Greens, 148
    Stir-Fried Beef with Asparagus,
        Bok Choy & Morels, 42
    Turkey Breast with Chanterelle
        Ragout, 107

N

Naked Carrot Cake with Spring
    Blossoms, 48
Nectarines
    Grilled Salmon with Stone Fruit–Herb
        Mojo, 72
    Watermelon, Nectarine & Mint Salad
        with Feta Cheese, 69
Noodles
    Noodle Bowl with Soy-Glazed Duck,
        Shiitake Mushrooms & Winter
        Greens, 148
    Rice-Noodle Salad with Chicken,
        Summer Vegetables & Herbs, 66
    Sesame-Ginger Noodles with Peas,
        Shaved Asparagus & Radishes, 39
Nuts
    Almond Tart Dough, 166
    Apricot Pistachio Tart, 82
    Fig, Blue Cheese & Walnut Crostini
        with Honey Drizzle, 92
    Pasta with Brussels Sprout Leaves,
        Hazelnuts & Brown Butter, 146
    Pear + Walnut Galette, 87
    Pomegranate + Walnut Toast, 51
    Rhubarb-Ginger Crumble with
        Cardamom Cream, 47
    Romaine & Roasted Delicata Squash
        Salad with Dates, Almonds
        & Bacon, 100

Walnut Torte with Chocolate-Caramel
    Sauce, 156

O

Olives
    Olive-Caper Gremolata, 99
    Pappardelle with Romaneso
        & Kalamata Olives, 102
Omelet-Soufflé with Spinach,
    Leek & New Potatoes, 33
Onions
    Cider-Braised Chicken Legs with
        Fresh Figs & Cipollini Onions, 116
    Pickled Onion, 56
Oranges
    Citrus Galette, 87
    Crème Brûlée with Caramelized
        Blood Oranges, 158
    Mixed Citrus Salad with Mâche,
        Fennel & Celery, 140
    Watermelon Radish Salad with
        Herbed Cheese, Blood Orange
        & Chives, 18
Orecchiette with Spring Vegetables,
    Pecorino & Prosciutto, 31
Oven-Roasted Ricotta with Citrus
    & Pomegranate, 132
Oysters, Roasted, with Sriracha-Lime
    Butter, 128

P

Panna Cotta, Kiwi & Passion Fruit, 46
Pan-Seared Salmon with Fresh Favas
    & Arugula Pesto, 37
Pan-Seared Sea Bass with
    Acorn Squash, 113
Pappardelle with Romaneso
    & Kalamata Olives, 102
Parsley
    Grilled Rib-Eye Steak with
        Avocado Chimichurri, 71
    Spring Herb Pesto, 43
Parsnip Oven Fries with Chile-Spiced
    Crème Fraîche, 135
Passion Fruit & Kiwi Panna Cotta, 46
Pasta
    Orecchiette with Spring Vegetables,
        Pecorino & Prosciutto, 31
    Pappardelle with Romaneso
        & Kalamata Olives, 102
    Pasta with Brussels Sprout Leaves,
        Hazelnuts & Brown Butter, 146
Pavlova with Meyer Lemon Curd
    & Strawberries, 45
Peaches
    Grilled Salmon with Stone Fruit–Herb
        Mojo, 72

Peach Flatbread with Burrata,
    Arugula & Pickled Onion, 56
Stone Fruit Salad with Summer
    Lettuces, Hazelnuts
    & Goat Cheese, 68
Pears
    The Hayride, 160
    Pear, Quince & Apple Galette, 119
    Pear + Walnut Galette, 87
    Salted Caramel–Dipped Pears, 154
    Wheat Berry Salad with Chopped
        Chard, Pear & Sunflower Seeds, 94
Peas
    Black Lentil Salad with Shrimp,
        Green Garlic, Snap Peas
        & Moroccan Vinaigrette, 28
    English Pea & Watercress Soup, 23
    Orecchiette with Spring Vegetables,
        Pecorino & Prosciutto, 31
    Pea + Radish Toast, 50
    Radish + Pea Salad, 122
    Ricotta & Pea Crostini with Tarragon
        & Pink Peppercorns, 20
    Seared Miso-Glazed Scallops with
        Snow Peas & Green Garlic, 38
    Sesame-Ginger Noodles with Peas,
        Shaved Asparagus & Radishes, 39
    types of, 34–35
Peppers
    Blistered Padrón Peppers with
        Spicy Garlic Aioli, 60
    Golden Gazpacho with Torn Croutons
        & Cherry Tomato Salsa, 61
    Mango, Green Onion & Mint Salsa, 151
    Pounded Chicken Breasts with
        Grilled Ratatouille, 79
    Rice-Noodle Salad with Chicken,
        Summer Vegetables & Herbs, 66
    Summer Vegetable Ceviche, 55
Persimmon, Fuyu, Salad with
    Endive & Pomegranate, 142
Pesto
    Arugula Pesto, 37
    Spring Herb Pesto, 43
Pineapple Salsa, 76
Pink Grapefruit Sorbet with
    Crystallized Ginger, 157
Pistachio Apricot Tart, 82
Pizza with Roasted Broccolini,
    Pancetta & Pine Nuts, 145
Plums
    Grilled Pork Chops with Summer
        Plums & Thyme, 78
    Grilled Salmon with Stone Fruit–Herb
        Mojo, 72
    Stone Fruit Salad with Summer
        Lettuces, Hazelnuts
        & Goat Cheese, 68

Polenta Parmesan, Creamy, with
Wild Mushrooms, 91
Pomegranate
Fuyu Persimmon Salad with
Endive & Pomegranate, 142
Oven-Roasted Ricotta with
Citrus & Pomegranate, 132
Pomegranate + Walnut Toast, 51
Roasted Pork Shoulder with Sweet
Potatoes & Pomegranate, 111
Pops, Watermelon Mojito, 84
Pork. See also Bacon & pancetta;
Prosciutto
Five-Spice Pork Loin with Mango,
Green Onion & Mint Salsa, 151
Grilled Pork Chops with Summer
Plums & Thyme, 78
Kale, White Bean & Sausage Soup, 97
Pork Skewers with Apple, Fresh Sage
& Rustic Bread, 108
Roasted Pork Shoulder with Sweet
Potatoes & Pomegranate, 111
Potatoes
Beef Tenderloin with Celery Root–
Potato Purée, 150
Omelet-Soufflé with Spinach,
Leek & New Potatoes, 33
Potato & Pancetta Crostata with
Fresh Rosemary, 133
Roasted Pork Shoulder with Sweet
Potatoes & Pomegranate, 111
Potpies, Blackberry & Blueberry, 81
Pounded Chicken Breasts with
Grilled Ratatouille, 79
Prosciutto
Mushroom Soup with Crispy
Prosciutto & Marjoram, 138
Orecchiette with Spring Vegetables,
Pecorino & Prosciutto, 31
Warm Kale Salad with Lentils
& Prosciutto, 143
Pumpkin
Pumpkin Purée, 167
Pumpkin Tart with
Gingersnap Crust, 120
Soft Tacos with Pumpkin,
Black Beans & Avocado, 101

Q
Quince, Pear & Apple Galette, 119

R
Radicchio, Smoked Trout & Horseradish
Cream, Crostini with, 129
Radishes
Pea + Radish Toast, 50
Radish + Pea Salad, 122

Rhubarb-Mint-Radish Slaw, 40
Sesame-Ginger Noodles with Peas,
Shaved Asparagus & Radishes, 39
Relish, Spicy Cranberry, 153
Rhubarb-Ginger Crumble with
Cardamom Cream, 47
Rhubarb-Mint-Radish Slaw, 40
Rice. See Risotto
Rice-Noodle Salad with Chicken,
Summer Vegetables & Herbs, 66
Ricotta & Pea Crostini with Tarragon
& Pink Peppercorns, 20
Risotto with Fresh Corn & Basil Oil, 65
Roasted Figs with Mascarpone, 121
Roasted Oysters with Sriracha-Lime
Butter, 128
Roasted Pork Shoulder with Sweet
Potatoes & Pomegranate, 111
Roasted Red & Yellow Beets with
Burrata, Sherry Vinaigrette &
Escarole, 127
Romaine & Roasted Delicata Squash
Salad with Dates, Almonds
& Bacon, 100
Romaneso & Kalamata Olives,
Pappardelle with, 102
Rum
Cranberry Daiquiri, 160
Mint Mojito, 161
Watermelon Mojito Pops, 84

S
Sage
Mushroom + Sage Toast, 51
Pork Skewers with Apple, Fresh Sage
& Rustic Bread, 108
Salads
Artichoke, Celery & Fennel Salad, 29
Black Lentil Salad with Shrimp, Green
Garlic, Snap Peas & Moroccan
Vinaigrette, 28
Chile-Spiced Halibut with Frisée
& Tangerine Salad, 147
Farro, Grilled Corn & Summer Squash
Salad, 64
Fuyu Persimmon Salad with Endive
& Pomegranate, 142
Little Gem Salad with Shaved
Carrot, Sunflower Seeds
& Dill Vinaigrette, 26
Mixed Citrus Salad with Mâche,
Fennel & Celery, 140
Rice-Noodle Salad with Chicken,
Summer Vegetables & Herbs, 66
Roasted Red & Yellow Beets with
Burrata, Sherry Vinaigrette
& Escarole, 127

Romaine & Roasted Delicata Squash
Salad with Dates, Almonds
& Bacon, 100
Sesame-Ginger Noodles with Peas,
Shaved Asparagus & Radishes, 39
Stone Fruit Salad with Summer Lettuces,
Hazelnuts & Goat Cheese, 68
Thai Beef Salad with Cucumber, Chile
& Greens, 63
Warm Kale Salad with Lentils
& Prosciutto, 143
Watermelon, Nectarine & Mint Salad
with Feta Cheese, 69
Watermelon Radish Salad with
Herbed Cheese, Blood Orange
& Chives, 18
Wheat Berry Salad with Chopped
Chard, Pear & Sunflower Seeds, 94
Salads for Every Season, 122–123
Salmon
Grilled Salmon with Stone Fruit–Herb
Mojo, 72
Pan-Seared Salmon with Fresh Favas
& Arugula Pesto, 37
Salsa
Cherry Tomato Salsa, 61
Mango, Green Onion & Mint Salsa, 151
Pineapple Salsa, 76
Salted Caramel–Dipped Pears, 154
Sauces
Chocolate-Caramel Sauce, 156
Spicy Garlic Aioli, 60
Tomato Sauce, 166–67
Sausage, Kale & White Bean Soup, 97
Scallops, Seared Miso-Glazed, with
Snow Peas & Green Garlic, 38
Sea Bass, Pan-Seared, with Acorn
Squash, 113
Seared Cauliflower Steaks with
Olive-Caper Gremolata, 99
Seared Miso-Glazed Scallops with
Snow Peas & Green Garlic, 38
Sesame-Ginger Noodles with Peas,
Shaved Asparagus & Radishes, 39
Shellfish
Black Lentil Salad with Shrimp,
Green Garlic, Snap Peas
& Moroccan Vinaigrette, 28
Clams in Leek Broth with Parsley
Vinaigrette, 25
Crab Cioppino, 139
Fresh Spring Rolls with Crab, Mango,
Jicama & Haricots Verts, 24
Roasted Oysters with Sriracha-Lime
Butter, 128
Seared Miso-Glazed Scallops with
Snow Peas & Green Garlic, 38

Turmeric-Spiced Shrimp with Red
   Cabbage & Carrot Slaw, 105
Short Ribs with Carrot-Apple Purée, 110
Shrimp
   Black Lentil Salad with Shrimp,
      Green Garlic, Snap Peas &
      Moroccan Vinaigrette, 28
   Crab Cioppino, 139
   Turmeric-Spiced Shrimp with
      Red Cabbage & Carrot Slaw, 105
Slaws
   Red Cabbage & Carrot Slaw, 105
   Rhubarb-Mint-Radish Slaw, 40
Smoky Eggplant Dip with
   Cumin-Crusted Pita Chips, 93
Soft Tacos with Pumpkin, Black Beans
   & Avocado, 101
Sorbet, Pink Grapefruit, with
   Crystallized Ginger, 157
Soups
   Clams in Leek Broth with
      Parsley Vinaigrette, 25
   Coconut-Curry Butternut Squash
      Soup, 96
   Creamy Cauliflower Soup with
      Brussels Sprout Hash, 130
   English Pea & Watercress Soup, 23
   Golden Gazpacho with Torn Croutons
      & Cherry Tomato Salsa, 61
   Kale, White Bean & Sausage Soup, 97
   Mushroom Soup with Crispy
      Prosciutto & Marjoram, 138
Spinach, Leek & New Potatoes,
   Omelet-Soufflé with, 33
Spring Herb Pesto, 43
Spring Rolls, Fresh, with Crab, Mango,
   Jicama & Haricots Verts, 24
Squash. See also Zucchini
   autumnal, types of, 114–15
   Chard + Squash Salad, 123
   Chicken Tagine with Roasted Squash,
      Haricots Verts, Chickpeas
      & Cranberries, 106
   Coconut-Curry Butternut Squash
      Soup, 96
   Farro, Grilled Corn & Summer Squash
      Salad, 64
   Fried Squash Blossoms with
      Ricotta, 57
   Pan-Seared Sea Bass with
      Acorn Squash, 113
   Pumpkin Purée, 167
   Pumpkin Tart with
      Gingersnap Crust, 120
   Romaine & Roasted Delicata Squash
      Salad with Dates, Almonds
      & Bacon, 100

Soft Tacos with Pumpkin,
   Black Beans & Avocado, 101
Stir-Fried Beef with Asparagus,
   Bok Choy & Morels, 42
Stone Fruit Galette, 86
Stone Fruit Salad with Summer Lettuces,
   Hazelnuts & Goat Cheese, 68
Strawberries
   Pavlova with Meyer Lemon Curd
      & Strawberries, 45
   Strawberry + Mint Galette, 86
Summer Cherry Clafoutis, 83
Summer Vegetable Ceviche, 55
Sunflower seeds
   Little Gem Salad with Shaved
      Carrot, Sunflower Seeds
      & Dill Vinaigrette, 26
   Wheat Berry Salad with Chopped
      Chard, Pear & Sunflower Seeds, 94
Sweet Potatoes & Pomegranate,
   Roasted Pork Shoulder with, 111
Swiss chard
   Chard + Squash Salad, 123
   Swiss Chard & Spring Onion
      Frittata, 32
   Wheat Berry Salad with Chopped
      Chard, Pear & Sunflower Seeds, 94

T

Tacos
   Grilled Fish Tacos with Pineapple
      Salsa & Avocado Crema, 76
   Soft Tacos with Pumpkin,
      Black Beans & Avocado, 101
Tangerines
   Chile-Spiced Halibut with Frisée
      & Tangerine Salad, 147
   Spicy Cranberry Relish, 153
Tarts
   Heirloom Tomato Tart, 58
   Pear, Quince & Apple Galette, 119
   Potato & Pancetta Crostata with
      Fresh Rosemary, 133
   Pumpkin Tart with
      Gingersnap Crust, 120
Thai Beef Salad with Cucumber, Chile &
   Greens, 63
Thin-Crust Dough, 166
Toasts for Every Season, 50–51
Tomatoes
   Fresh Heirloom Tomato Sauce, 73
   Golden Gazpacho with Torn Croutons
      & Cherry Tomato Salsa, 61
   Green Bean + Cherry Tomato
      Salad, 122
   Heirloom Tomato Tart, 58

Tomato + Basil Toast, 50
Tomato Sauce, 166–67
Trout, Smoked, Radicchio, & Horseradish
   Cream, Crostini with, 129
Turkey Breast with Chanterelle
   Ragout, 107
Turmeric-Spiced Shrimp with
   Red Cabbage & Carrot Slaw, 105

V

Vegetables. See also specific vegetables
   fall, 165
   spring and summer, 164
   winter, 136–37, 165

W

Walnuts
   Fig, Blue Cheese & Walnut Crostini
      with Honey Drizzle, 92
   Pear + Walnut Galette, 87
   Pomegranate + Walnut Toast, 51
   Walnut Torte with Chocolate-Caramel
      Sauce, 156
Warm Kale Salad with Lentils
   & Prosciutto, 143
Watercress & English Pea Soup, 23
Watermelon, Nectarine & Mint Salad
   with Feta Cheese, 69
Watermelon Mojito Pops, 84
Watermelon Radish Salad with Herbed
   Cheese, Blood Orange & Chives, 18
Wheat Berry Salad with Chopped Chard,
   Pear & Sunflower Seeds, 94
Whipped cream
   Cardamom Cream, 47
   Cinnamon Cream, 117

Z

Zucchini
   Farro, Grilled Corn & Summer Squash
      Salad, 64
   Pounded Chicken Breasts with
      Grilled Ratatouille, 79
   Rice-Noodle Salad with Chicken,
      Summer Vegetables & Herbs, 66
   Summer Vegetable Ceviche, 55
   Zucchini Lasagna with Herbed Ricotta
      & Fresh Heirloom Tomato Sauce, 73

weldon**owen**

Weldon Owen is a division of Bonnier Publishing USA
1045 Sansome Street, Suite 100, San Francisco, CA 94111
www.weldonowen.com

WELDON OWEN, INC.

President & Publisher Roger Shaw
SVP, Sales & Marketing Amy Kaneko

Associate Publisher Amy Marr
Senior Editor Lisa Atwood

Creative Director Kelly Booth
Art Director Marisa Kwek
Senior Production Designer Rachel Lopez Metzger

Associate Production Director Michelle Duggan
Imaging Manager Don Hill

Photographer Ray Kachatorian
Food Stylist Valerie Aikman-Smith
Prop Stylist Jennifer Barguiarena

COOKING IN SEASON

Conceived and produced by
Weldon Owen, Inc.
In collaboration with
Williams Sonoma, Inc.
3250 Van Ness Avenue
San Francisco, CA 94109

A WELDON OWEN PRODUCTION
Copyright © 2017 Weldon Owen, Inc.
and Williams Sonoma, Inc.
All rights reserved, including the
right of reproduction in whole or
in part in any form.

Library of Congress
Cataloging-in-Publication
data is available.

ISBN: 978-1-68188-257-4

Printed and bound in China

First printed in 2017
10 9 8 7 6 5 4 3 2 1

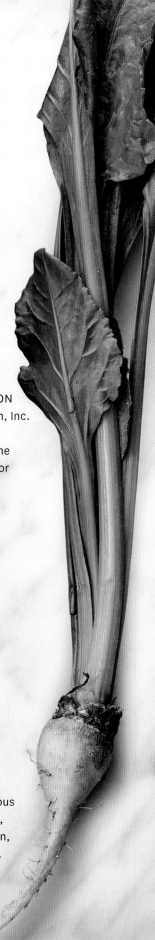

ACKNOWLEDGMENTS

Weldon Owen wishes to thank the following people for their generous
support in producing this book: Kris Balloun, Lesley Bruynesteyn,
Amanda Fredrickson, Gloria Geller, Carolyn Miller, Elizabeth Parson,
Michelle Reiner, Sharon Silva, Toven Stith, and Sandra Tripicchio.

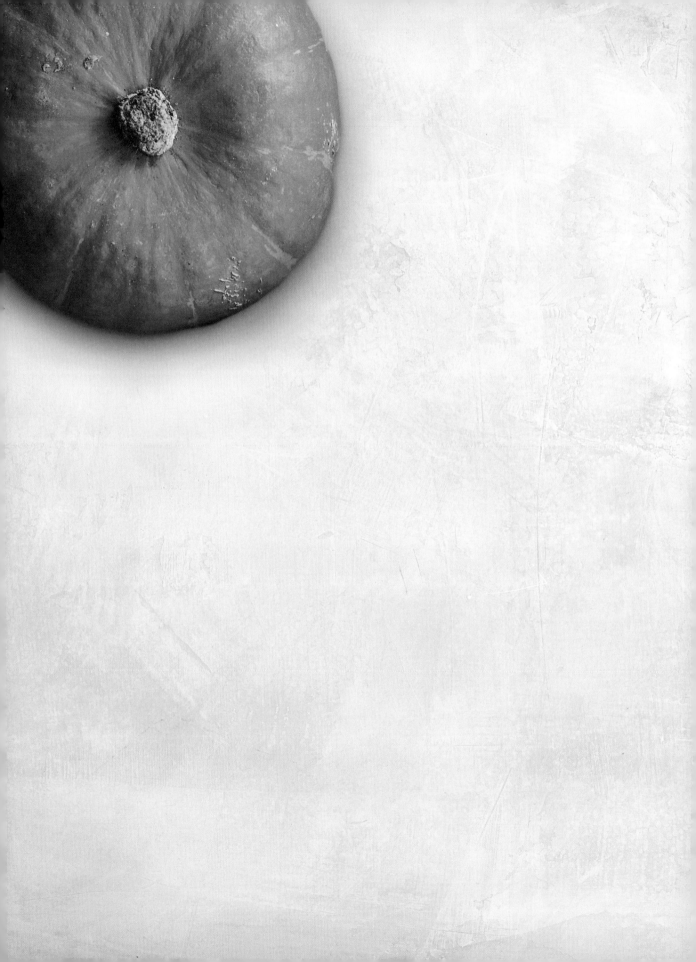